BMW M5

The Complete Story

OTHER TITLES IN THE CROWOOD AUTOCLASSICS SERIES

ALFA ROMEO 916 GTV AND SPIDER Robert Foskett

ALFA ROMEO SPIDER John Tipler

ASTON MARTIN DB4, DB5 & DB6 Jonathan Wood

ASTON MARTIN DB7 Andrew Noakes

ASTON MARTIN V8 William Presland

AUDI QUATTRO Laurence Meredith

AUSTIN HEALEY Graham Robson

BMW 5 SERIES James Taylor

BMW CLASSIC COUPÉS James Taylor

BMW M3 James Taylor

CITROËN DS SERIES John Pressnell

FERRARI 308, 328 AND 348 Robert Foskett

FORD ESCORT RS Graham Robson

FROGEYE SPRITE John Baggott

JAGUAR E-TYPE Jonathan Wood

JAGUAR XK8 Graham Robson

JENSEN INTERCEPTOR John Tipler

JOWETT JAVELIN AND JUPITER Geoff McAuley & Edmund Nankivell

LAMBORGHINI COUNTACH Peter Dron

LAND ROVER DEFENDER, 90 AND 110 RANGE James Taylor

LOTUS ELAN Matthew Vale

MGA David G. Styles

MGB Brian Laban

MGF AND TF David Knowles

MG T-SERIES Graham Robson

MAZDA MX-5 Antony Ingram

MERCEDES-BENZ CARS OF THE 1990s James Taylor

MERCEDES-BENZ 'FINTAIL' MODELS Brian Long

MERCEDES-BENZ S-CLASS James Taylor

MERCEDES-BENZ W124 James Taylor

MERCEDES SL SERIES Andrew Noakes

MERCEDES W113 Myles Kornblatt

MORGAN 4/4 Michael Palmer

MORGAN THREE-WHEELER Peter Miller

PEUGEOT 205 Adam Sloman

PORSCHE CARRERA – THE AIR-COOLED ERA Johnny Tipler

RELIANT THREE-WHEELERS John Wilson-Hall

RILEY RM John Price-Williams

ROVER 75 AND MG ZT James Taylor

ROVER P5 & P5B James Taylor

SAAB 99 & 900 Lance Cole

SHELBY & AC COBRA Brian Laban

SUBARU IMPREZA WRX AND WRX STI James Taylor

SUNBEAM ALPINE AND TIGER Graham Robson

TOYOTA MR2 Nigel Burton

TRIUMPH SPITFIRE & GT6 Richard Dredge

TRIUMPH TR7 David Knowles

TVR – THE CARS OF THE PETER WHEELER ERA Ralph Dodds

VOLKSWAGEN GOLF GTI James Richardson

VOLVO P1800 David G. Styles

BMW M5

The Complete Story

James Taylor

THE CROWOOD PRESS

First published in 2015 by
The Crowood Press Ltd
Ramsbury, Marlborough
Wiltshire SN8 2HR

www.crowood.com

© James Taylor 2015

All rights reserved. No part of this publication may be reproduced or transmitted in any form or by any means, electronic or mechanical, including photocopy, recording, or any information storage and retrieval system, without permission in writing from the publishers.

British Library Cataloguing-in-Publication Data
A catalogue record for this book is available from the British Library.

ISBN 978 1 78500 045 4

Typeset by Jean Cussons Typesetting, Diss, Norfolk

Printed and bound in India by Replika Press Pvt Ltd

CONTENTS

	Introduction and Acknowledgements	6
CHAPTER 1	THE M5 IN CONTEXT	7
CHAPTER 2	THE E28 M5 (1984–1987)	23
CHAPTER 3	THE 3.6-LITRE E34 M5	45
CHAPTER 4	THE 3.8-LITRE E34 M5	65
CHAPTER 5	E39 M5 – THE FIRST V8	84
CHAPTER 6	THE E60 AND E61 V10 MODELS	104
CHAPTER 7	THE F10 TURBOCHARGED CARS	134
CHAPTER 8	SO YOU THINK YOU WANT AN M5?	157
	Index	174

INTRODUCTION AND ACKNOWLEDGEMENTS

This book is intended as a companion volume to the one I wrote a year or so ago on the M3 models. It has been a very rewarding book to write, although a little frustrating at times when information proved to be unavailable, or to be available in multiple conflicting versions!

The M5 has always been one of my very favourite cars – a relatively ordinary-looking four-door saloon with the acceleration of a supercar and (in most cases) a cocoon of luxury and high equipment levels as well. What more could you want from your everyday transport? Well … affordability, perhaps. That was one reason why I never did follow up that very tempting but slightly unloved E34 3.6-litre model I looked over at Munich Legends a few years ago. Sadly, things like mortgages and children tend to demand both money and time!

However, for those blissfully unencumbered by such worries, I hope this book will provide the essential background to their enjoyment of one of the world's most complete cars. I have tried to explain not only the What but also the Why and the How as a way of illuminating the essence of these cars and explaining why they are so appealing.

As for the M3 book, my friend Nick Dimbleby rediscovered some splendid pictures he had taken of M5s, and many of those illustrate the E28 and E34 chapters of this book. Many other pictures have reached me through BMW GB and BMW in Germany, South Africa and the USA, all of whom helped with information in some areas. Photographers Dave Smith and Dominic Fraser provided some top-quality photographs, and Munich Legends kindly allowed me to take pictures of cars they had in stock. Some pictures have come from Wikimedia Commons, and I'm grateful to the enthusiasts who have made them available for use in a publication like this; those photographs are individually acknowledged in the text. Special thanks go to Bob Harper at *BMW Car* magazine and to Richard and Vicky Dredge at Magic Car Pics for finding pictures I couldn't source elsewhere, and at zero notice. I'm grateful, too, to Barbara Cleveland at Brooklands Books for allowing me to plunder that company's massive library of magazine articles for information.

I'll make one other point before you get into the meat of the book. We have used the title of *BMW M5 – The Complete Story* because it fits in with a series produced by Crowood Publishing. The story is as complete as I can make it, but it goes only up to the end of 2014. There will be more to tell one day, because the M5 remains in production, and I hope I will be able to update this book with more of the story when the time comes.

James Taylor
Oxfordshire, February 2015

CHAPTER ONE

THE M5 IN CONTEXT

So what exactly is a BMW M5? Defining it as an ultra-high-performance medium-sized saloon car made by BMW really tells very little of the story, because the M5 has become something of an automotive legend. Today, the very name of M5 evokes a whole set of responses from motoring enthusiasts, but among them are invariably ideas of luxury, exclusivity, prestige, excitement and fun. That the latter two play a big part in the reasons BMW sells its M5 in such large quantities is encapsulated in a devastatingly accurate if slightly tongue-in-cheek comment made in *Evo* magazine for October 2011: 'The main reason the M5 exists is to bait sports car drivers, avoid the law and keep the driver amused.'

Even though the M5 set the precedent for other car makers to follow, it was not in itself the first high-performance saloon car. Long before its introduction in 1984, specialist tuning companies in Germany had been creating saloon cars with sports-car performance and handling by modifying existing production models. The two leading companies in the field were Alpina, who had focused on BMW products from the mid-1960s, and AMG, who worked on Mercedes-Benz models from 1968. Their cars were subtle (unless the customers demanded otherwise), superbly engineered, and formidably expensive.

Yet these largely bespoke and relatively rare creations made clear that high performance need not be limited to an impractical, two-seater sports car. They awakened the interest of many potential buyers who needed a four-door saloon for family and work commitments, but did not want

These are the five generations of M5 covered in the current book. From left to right in the back row are the E28, E34, E39 and E60, and in the foreground is the F10 model. BMW

7

■ THE M5 IN CONTEXT

This image dates from the 1980s, when the Motorsport division was becoming established as a builder of high-performance road cars. Below the M logo, it claims that M is 'the strongest letter in the world', and at the bottom describes the Motorsport division as a 'trend-setter in the high-performance league'. BMW

The M cars were not the first high-performance BMW saloons; specialist tuners had got there first, and the most respected of them was Alpina. This is a 1987 Alpina B7 Turbo, which boasted 300PS – more than the E28 M5 of the day. ALPINA UK

Nor was BMW the only marque to benefit from the attentions of high-performance specialists. AMG's work with Mercedes-Benz went back to the late 1960s, and this is one of their mid-1980s offerings, contemporary with the original M5. MERCEDES-AMG

THE M5 IN CONTEXT

to sacrifice the performance and handling of the sports cars they might have enjoyed in younger days. Most importantly, many of them had reached a stage in life where they could afford to have such a machine built specially for them.

Even though Alpina was a small-volume operation, it was undeniably successful, and BMW enjoyed a close relationship with the company from the late 1960s, when Alpina began to field BMW cars in motor sport. Less visibly as far as the public was concerned, BMW itself also began in 1974 to make its own high-performance specials for VIP customers, using its Motorsport division to fit engines from its large cars (in those days the E3 saloons and E9 coupés) into the medium-sized E12 5 Series saloons. Brakes, suspension and other elements were uprated to suit, and the swept volume and outputs of those engines gradually rose as new versions were introduced in production. There were more of these 'Motorsport 5 Series' cars than is generally realized, and although no incontrovertible records survive, it is widely believed that 895 were built between 1974 and 1980 – an average of about 127 cars a year.

By the end of the 1970s, BMW senior management was beginning to wonder whether this sideline could be turned into a more mainstream profit-earning activity, and plans were put forward to begin regular production of a high-performance 5 Series derivative with a standardized specification. As before, the car would pass through the Motorsport division's workshops to be fitted with its high-performance components. However, there was a clear element of risk in this plan, because building a standardized car in quantity and trying to sell it was quite a different proposition from responding to VIP customer demand by building bespoke conversions.

Treading gingerly at first, BMW added the letter M to a high-performance version of the E12 saloon that was called the M535i. The deep front air dam gave away that this was a special version of the car, and the upholstery with its tricolour stripes can just be seen through the windscreen. BMW

9

■ THE M5 IN CONTEXT

The first M535i was a success, and was followed by an M535i version of the E28 models. This, though, was largely a cosmetic exercise ... the real thing was now ready for release. NICK DIMBLEBY

In South Africa, BMW satisfied the local market for a high-performance E28 with a special version of the M535i. South Africa would go on to play an interesting part in the story of the M5 models. BMW SOUTH AFRICA

So BMW moved cautiously at first, choosing to test the market with a Motorsport-prepared version of the E12 5 Series in that model's final year of production. It called this new model an M535i, the initial M signifying the involvement of the Motorsport division, and it entered production in April 1980, lasting until May 1981 (although versions built from completely knocked down (CKD) kits in South Africa were available for longer). The M535i boasted the most powerful version then available of the M30 'big-block six' engine, a 3.5-litre size, which was otherwise found only in the big 735i saloons and the 635CSi coupés. The cars were built from partially assembled 5 Series models that were taken from the main assembly lines at Dingolfing and com-

pleted by the Motorsport division at Garching. Customer response was very promising, and BMW decided to field an M535i again as part of its new E28 5 Series range that was introduced in 1981.

This second M535i was not introduced until autumn 1984, and it benefited from BMW's experience with the first version. The E12 M535i had been supplied uniquely in white and sometimes had racing stripes in the BMW Motorsport colours – fashionable for the time, perhaps, but not really what the customers wanted. So the E28 M535i was visually toned down, and was recognizable only by its special body-kit of spoilers and sill extensions, and by its special wheels. Under the bonnet once again

THE M5 IN CONTEXT

was BMW's largest and most powerful 6-cylinder engine, although in this case that same engine was also available in the mainstream 535i model. Otherwise, the car's only special features were a more sporty suspension and sports-oriented front seats. These models were not completed by the Motorsport division, but were built with all the mainstream E28 models on the assembly lines in Dingolfing.

This second M535i, however, had a rather different purpose from the first. It was intended as a curtain-raiser for a proper Motorsport-developed car based on the E28 5 Series. As Chapter 2 explains, the date of the new model's announcement was arranged to cause maximum disruption during the launch period of the new Mercedes-Benz medium-sized saloon, but the first examples of the car were actually completed in October 1984, at the same time as the new M535i was announced. Rumours of an ultra-high-performance model were then allowed to circulate for a few months until the new M5 was revealed at the Amsterdam Motor Show in February 1985.

There was a huge difference between the M535i and the M5. Most important was that the M5 had been extensively re-developed by the Motorsport division, and it featured a version of the 3.5-litre M88 engine that had been seen in the M1 supercar at the end of the 1970s. Suspension, brakes and steering had all come in for attention, too. Unlike the M535i, which in E28 guise was largely a cosmetic exercise, this was the real deal. In line with customers' wishes, it was also discreet, and although it had spoilers both front and rear to improve its high-speed aerodynamics, these were nowhere near as brash as those on the M535i. The M5 was a car that would barely attract a second glance from the man in the street; in every sense of the word, it was a car for the *cognoscenti*.

BMW has always been keen to draw on its heritage. This picture was taken to publicize the first versions of the E34 M5, seen in the foreground. Behind it is an E28 M5, and in the background the red car is an M1, the first road-going production car from the Motorsport division. BMW

11

■ THE M5 IN CONTEXT

THE M5 AND MOTOR SPORT

Even though the M5 came from the Motorsport division of BMW, it was never promoted as a competition machine. That task was largely left to the smaller M3, which from 1986 took over the duty of upholding the BMW name in touring-car racing from the 2002 models and went on to become the most successful touring-car racer of all time. BMW did look at creating a racing version of the M5 sometime around 2005, as Chapter 7 explains, but nothing came of it.

Nevertheless, some privateers have campaigned M5s. Former Formula 1 champion Alan Jones led a team that raced an E34 model in the 1992 Bathurst 12-Hour Production Car endurance race in Australia, and finished first in class and second overall. Then between 1997 and 2005, André Carlier campaigned an E34 M5 in the Belcar Championship (the Belgian national sports-car series) with some success.

LEFT: **The Motorsport division of course had a long and distinguished record in competition, as this advertisement from the 1970s makes clear.** BMW

The smaller M3 models upheld the BMW name in track events, but the M5 never represented the factory in touring-car racing. BMW

THE M5 IN CONTEXT

That first M5 has since been followed by four more cars with the M5 name, each one based on the latest generation of BMW's medium-sized 5 Series saloons and each one discussed in more detail later in this book. Note that although there have now been six generations of 5 Series – E12, E28, E34, E39, E60 and F10 – there have only been five generations of M5, because there was no M5 derivative of the E12 range. Over those five generations, the M5 has not only become a legend of its own, but was also responsible for kick-starting the whole BMW M phenomenon. Today there are high-performance M derivatives of most of the BMW model-ranges and the M brand is a major generator of revenue for its parent company as well as a valuable ingredient in its high-quality, high-performance brand image.

ABOVE: **The tail badge of the M1 pioneered the device of the letter M with the tricolour Motorsport stripes still in use today.** BMW

BELOW: **A special ProCar racing series was organized to showcase the BMW M1. Here, the cars are seen in the curtain-raiser event for the Grand Prix in Monaco.** BMW

■ THE M5 IN CONTEXT

The M1 set the scene and in many ways tested the capabilities of the Motorsport division, but it was also a blind alley in development. Only its engine continued in later M models, and even then after much modification. BMW

THE M5 OVER THE YEARS

The most special feature of every M5 has always been its engine, even though the Motorsport division has always developed the suspension, steering and brakes as well so that the high-performance 5 Series is a fully balanced and properly engineered car rather than a mere conversion of the mainstream production model.

In the beginning, the E28 M5 came with a road-going derivative of the M88 engine developed by the Motorsport division for the M1 supercar. This was a 6-cylinder engine with four valves per cylinder, and with 286PS in European form (power was less with the catalytic converter required in North America) was phenomenally powerful for its time. It was also so far ahead of potential rivals from the major car manufacturers that there was no need to do much more than uprate it a little with a longer stroke for the second-generation M5 in 1988. So the E34 version of the M5 had 315PS, despite the power-sapping effect of its standard catalytic converter, and that was enough to keep BMW ahead of the game until 1990 when, as Chapter 4 explains, some serious opposition surfaced from Mercedes-Benz and Opel.

BMW's response was to re-engine the E34 M5 with a larger-capacity 3.8-litre version of the 24-valve 6-cylinder (known as an S38 since it had been fitted with catalytic converters), now delivering 340PS. The company also decided to make the M5 available with a second body style to ensure it still had a product that was not rivalled by other makers, and a Touring estate version of the 3.8-litre E34 reached the showrooms in 1992. By this stage, however, it was clear that the S38 6-cylinder engine had reached the limit of its development, and for the next M5 there would have to be a completely new engine. The threat of change did not sit easily with enthusiasts of the M brand, many of them devoted to the smooth and refined power delivery of the Motorsport 'six'.

It was inevitable that the replacement engine should be a V8. BMW had already developed a range of V8 petrol engines for its top models, and these made their appearance in 1992. Further-developed versions arrived two years later, and it was from the larger-capacity version of these

THE M5 IN CONTEXT

TOP: **Alpina** meanwhile continued to produce formidable upgrades of the **BMW** saloons, and this one was a B10 model built for the **UK** in 1988. Alpina conversions were expensive, often more bespoke than the M cars, and qualitatively different. ALPINA UK

BELOW: **The second-generation M5 was derived from the E34 model 5 Series. Although this is a US publicity picture, the car is actually a European-specification model without the side marker lights demanded by North American regulations.** BMW NORTH AMERICA

15

■ THE M5 IN CONTEXT

Caught on the hop by rival cars from Mercedes-Benz and Opel, BMW re-engined the E34 M5 to keep it competitive. This is one of the later 3.8-litre models. BMW

that BMW M developed its next M5 engine. Nevertheless, it was not until 1998 that the third-generation or E39 version of the M5 entered production. The mainstream versions of the E39 5 Series saloons had already been on sale for nearly three years, but the delay may not have been caused entirely by the need to develop a new engine. As Chapter 5 explains, the launch date of the E39 M5 may well have been chosen to cause maximum disruption to Mercedes-Benz product plans again.

By this stage, BMW was well aware that it could sell all the M5s it could make, and that the assembly facilities at its Motorsport plant in Garching were too small to meet likely demand. So the E39 M5 was designed to be assembled with the mainstream E39 models on the production lines in Dingolfing – using, of course, components designed by BMW M. The E34 M5s were therefore the last of the M5s to be completed by hand, and the new M5s were volume-produced cars. That made them no less exclusive than before, however, and the new V8 engine – enlarged to a capacity of nearly 5 litres to compete on size at least with the rival Mercedes-Benz E500 saloon – delivered a huge 400PS to give blistering acceleration.

For the next iteration of the M5, however, BMW took a different approach. As Chapter 6 suggests, BMW felt for a

The UK was always a very strong market for the M5, and this is a UK-market version of the third-generation of E39 model. BMW UK

16

THE M5 IN CONTEXT

There had been an estate ('Touring') version of the E34 M5, and although no estate version of the E39 entered production, **BMW** did field an estate version of the fourth-generation M5. This was an E61 (the saloon was an E60), but was not a strong seller. BMW

The fifth-generation M5 was the F10. Here it is as a 30 Jahre M5 Edition, celebrating thirty years of the M5 in 2014. This special edition had a massive 600PS from its twin-turbocharged V8 engine. BMW

17

■ THE M5 IN CONTEXT

number of reasons that a larger-capacity engine was not the way forward. So it focused on a completely new V10 engine, loosely inspired by the BMW V10 engines used in Formula 1 racing and able to provide a V8 derivative for the M3 models as well. The V10 engine arrived in the fourth-generation or E60 M5 in 2004, and in a Touring estate (E61) version of the same car introduced in 2007 to compete against high-performance estates from rival makers. It was a formidably complicated and high-revving power unit that, as always, delivered what M5 buyers wanted – this time, 500PS. Controversial in its time, the V10 was nevertheless nowhere near as controversial as the engine that followed it in the fifth-generation M5.

That fifth-generation car arrived in 2011 as a derivative of the F10 or sixth-generation 5 Series. This time, there would be no Touring derivative, as the estate models of the previous M5 range had not been strong sellers. The general trend in the motor industry during the first decade of the twenty-first century was to downsize engines as a way of reducing fuel consumption and exhaust emissions, and BMW achieved this for the M5 by using a smaller-capacity engine than before and adding turbochargers – a first on an engine from the M division. The new engine was again a V8, developed from the mainstream BMW engine of the same 4.4-litre capacity, but making full use of twin turbochargers to provide the torque delivery and acceleration expected in an M5. This engine delivered no less than 560PS – 10 per cent more than the V10 it replaced – and in a special edition M5 released in 2012 revealed that it could be tuned to deliver as much as 600PS.

At the time of writing, BMW is no doubt already developing its sixth-generation M5, and of course a new engine will be central to it. Speculation is always prone to becoming outdated overnight, but it might not be fanciful to suggest that the next M5 engine could run on diesel fuel. Spectacular progress has been made in the last decade or so with diesel engines, and the best ones excel in fuel consumption (an important consideration today, even for an M5) and in torque delivery, which of course provides the acceleration that is fundamental to the M5 ethos. Maximum speed is, after all, less of a consideration at a time when Germany's top saloons are governed to a maximum of 250km/h (155mph) and increasing numbers of mainstream cars can reach that speed with ease.

The importance of North America

It is easy to imagine that the majority of M5s have always been sold in their native Germany, where long stretches of

From very early on, the USA was identified as a major potential market for the M5, and it has taken more examples of the cars than any other. This is a US-specification E28 M5, with the impact-absorbing bumpers and side marker lights required in that country.
BMW NORTH AMERICA

18

THE M5 IN CONTEXT

The worldwide success of the M division has led to a proliferation of other M models. This is a 2014 M6 coupé, based on the 6 Series cars ... BMW

AN M5 TIMELINE

1984 (October)	Production begins of the E28 M5
1986 (November)	First M5s (E28 models) for North America
1988 (June)	Last E28 M5s built in Germany
1988 (September)	Production begins (in Germany) of the E34 M5
1988 (November)	Last E28 M5s assembled in South Africa
1991 (November)	Last E34 3.6-litre M5 for Europe
	First 3.8-litre E34 M5 built
1992 (March)	Production begins of the E34 M5 Touring
1993 (March)	Last E34 M5 (3.6-litre) for North America
1995 (July)	Last E34 M5 built
1998 (October)	Production begins of the E39 M5
2003 (June)	Last E39 M5 built
2004 (September)	Production begins of the E60 M5
2007 (March)	Production begins of the E61 M5 Touring
2009 (December)	Last E60 M5 built
2010 (February)	Last E61 M5 Touring built
2011 (November)	Production begins of the F10 M5
2012 (March)	First F10 M5 models for North America

19

■ THE M5 IN CONTEXT

... and this is a 2014 **X6M**, much appreciated in the **USA** as a high-performance derivative of the **X6 SUV** model, but treated with caution in Europe where there is less enthusiasm for **SUVs**. BMW

FIVE GENERATIONS OF M5 – A PERFORMANCE COMPARISON

All figures are for European-specification saloons.

Model	PS	0–60mph	0–100km/h	Maximum	Derestricted maximum
E28	286	6.2 sec	7 sec	153mph (246km/h)	
E34 3.6	315	6.3 sec		155mph (250km/h)*	
E34 3.8	340	5.7 sec		155mph (250km/h)*	
E39	400	4.8 sec		155mph (250km/h)*	186mph (300km/h)
E60	500	4.8 sec		155mph (250km/h)*	205mph (330km/h)
F10	560	3.7 sec	4.3 sec	155mph (250km/h)*	205mph (330km/h)

* Electronically limited.

Autobahn without speed restrictions make their use at high speeds an everyday possibility. However, that is simply not the case; the biggest sales of M5s have actually been in North America, with the lion's share being made in the USA.

For that reason, the specification of every M5 has been carefully calculated to suit American market demands, even if it also suits European and other tastes as well. From the early days of the E28 M5, BMW has been prepared to build special models to suit US customer demand – and, of course, to avoid sending models to North America that its market research suggests will not sell well.

The trend was apparent from the earliest years of M5 production. Although production of the E28 M5 for North America did not begin until 1986, more than a year after production for Europe had got under way, the North American cars eventually accounted for well over half of all those built: 1,340 out of a total of 2,241, or about 60 per cent. The position was less clear-cut during the E34 era, when

BMW CAR AND ENGINE CODES

Car codes
Beginning in the early 1960s, BMW assigned a project code to each new car it prepared. Those codes had a number preceded by E, and that letter stood for Entwicklung, which is the German word for 'development'. This book refers in particular to the E28, E34, E39, E60 and E61 models, each of which gave rise to an M5 derivative.

Although a few of the early 1960s cars had three-figure numbers (the 2000C and 2000CS coupés, for example, were E120 types), at some point BMW decided not to go beyond 99 in its numbering system. The numbers were not used in strict ascending order, and not every number between 1 and 99 is known to have been used – although some could have been used for projects that did not prosper.

Once the sequence of E numbers had been exhausted, BMW decided to start a new numbering sequence beginning with F, which appears not to stand for anything in particular but is simply the next letter of the alphabet after E. The first of these new projects was the F01 7 Series model that entered production in 2008. So far, the only F code associated with the M5 is F10, which was for the sixth-generation 5 Series that entered production in 2009.

Engine codes
From the 1960s, BMW gave each of its engines an alphanumeric code beginning with the letter M. This stood for Motor, the German word for engine. As with its car projects, the company decided not to go beyond 99 in the numbering sequence, and from about 2001 most new engine projects were prefixed with the letter N. Like the F in the car codes, this was simply the next letter of the alphabet after the one already in use.

The engines built by the Motorsport division originally had numbers in the M sequence, a notable example relevant to this book being the M88. However, from 1986, Motorsport engines were given their own type numbering sequence with an S prefix (which stood for Sport, the same word in both German and English). The first engine to carry this was the S38, a version of the M88 developed for the US market with catalytic converters. All subsequent Motorsport engines have included a suffix that indicates their swept volume. In this book, there are references to the S38B35 (i.e. 3.5-litre), S38B38 (i.e. 3.8-litre), S62B50, S85B50 and S63B44TU. That TU suffix is a further recent addition that stands for Technical Update (BMW has taken to using American English in many areas, and this is an example). In cases where the M division engine is derived from a standard production engine, the S prefix is added to the number used for that engine, so the S62 is derived from the M62 and the S63 from the N63.

There have additionally been other engine prefix codes, but these have not been relevant to the M division's cars. Early BMW Minis had engines with a W prefix, while the new modular 3-cylinder engine family introduced in 2013 for the Mini and the i8 hybrid sports car has a B prefix.

■ THE M5 IN CONTEXT

> ### A CHANGE OF NAME
>
> BMW Motorsport GmbH changed its name to BMW M GmbH in 1993, just after the last E34 M5 models had been built for North America.
>
> There were several business reasons for the change, but one was undoubtedly the strength of the M brand. Another was that BMW had longer-term plans to give the M division a wider remit. In future, it would be responsible not only for motor-sport activities but also for much of the bespoke work on production vehicles – including, of course, the M5 itself.

BMW's M5 sales took a battering from the new Mercedes-Benz models in the USA and the later 3.8-litre cars were not homologated for North American sales at all. Even then, North America took 1,691 examples of the 8,383 3.6-litre cars built, or a healthy 20 per cent.

The position was largely restored with the E39 models, when North America took 9,992 of the 20,482 cars built, which works out as about 49 per cent of the total. Of the E60s that followed them, there were 9,491 for North America out of 20,589, or just over 46 per cent. It is too early yet to give figures for the F10 models, but there is no reason not to suppose that North American sales will account for a little less than half of all the cars eventually produced.

> ### THE M5 'RING TAXI'
>
> BMW does a lot of its high-speed testing at the Nürburgring, the race track high in the Eifel mountains between Cologne and Frankfurt in northern Germany. The Nordschleife (Northern Loop), built in the 1920s, is 12.9 miles (20.8km) long with 73 corners and has more than 1,000ft (300m) of elevation between its lowest and highest points. Much of the area around this track is forest.
>
> In 1986, BMW provided an M5 that would offer visitors to the Nürburgring high-speed rides around the track – driven, obviously, by a professional. The rides became so popular that the tradition continues to this day, although of course that original M5 'Ring Taxi' has been superseded by later M5s.
>
> From BMW's point of view, the Ring Taxi works as a very effective public relations tool, demonstrating the performance and handling of its flagship performance machine while also giving passengers the chance to experience the Nordschleife, famously nicknamed as the 'Green Hell' by racing driver Jackie Stewart. By late 2014, the BMW Ring Taxi had taken more than 90,000 passengers around the circuit, covering more than 650,000km and 30,000 laps. However, even the best drivers make mistakes, and in August 2014 footage appeared on YouTube showing the Ring Taxi sliding into the safety barrier on a corner. Fortunately, nobody was seriously hurt in the incident – although no doubt somebody's pride took a dent.

CHAPTER TWO

THE E28 M5 (1984–1987)

It is at least arguable that the introduction of the first M5 was intended as a spoiler for the new Mercedes-Benz medium-sized saloon. In the early 1980s, BMW was still running second to Mercedes in the race for domestic German sales in the medium-sized saloon sector, but the Bavarian company had set its long-term sights on beating Mercedes at their own game, and much of its product strategy was aimed at that end result.

BMW had introduced its new 5 Series model in 1981, and this medium-sized saloon range was not due for replacement until 1988. Meanwhile, the Mercedes model-replacement cycle had reached a different stage, and the long-running W123 series cars were scheduled for replacement in 1984. BMW would have nothing new in the sector to counter this, and the new Mercedes was likely to make a sizeable dent in sales of the mid-range BMW. Unless BMW could steal some of its thunder.

History has not recorded whose idea it was to develop an ultra-high-performance version of BMW's own mid-range saloon to grab media attention at a time when Mercedes wanted it most. However, the idea was logical enough for it to have occurred to several members of BMW's top management at once. The key difference in approach between BMW and Mercedes in the early 1980s was that BMW focused far more on driving dynamics and high performance; Mercedes, somewhat unfairly, was always seen as more conventional and even a bit staid. So a new high-performance BMW was entirely in keeping with the BMW ethos, and if it were based on the medium-sized saloon that was the direct competitor for the new Mercedes, it would have maximum impact.

Realistically, nobody ever expected it to make much difference to Mercedes sales. But what it would do was raise the BMW profile at a time when Mercedes were hogging the headlines, and emphasize that difference of approach between the two companies. Better yet, it was achievable within the time-frame, and it would be a relatively low-budget operation. So the idea of the M5 was born.

THE E28 5 SERIES

BMW had begun work on the E28 saloon range in 1975, just three years after the first of the 5 Series cars (the E12 range) had entered production. At this stage, BMW was still a relatively small company and was still battling its way upwards from the difficult days just a decade and a half earlier when there had been every chance that it would be absorbed by Mercedes-Benz. So the company had to proceed with some caution, however bullish an image it projected to the outside world.

Replacing the medium-sized range was a big undertaking, and the whole project was overshadowed by the new worldwide emphasis on fuel economy that had followed the Oil Crisis of 1973–74. For the long-term future, BMW was planning a special economy version of its small 6-cylinder engine (this would arrive in 1982 as the 'eta' engine) as well as a diesel engine (which would arrive in 1984), but for the moment the focus had to be on more readily achievable goals. So a great deal of effort was put into weight saving and improved aerodynamics.

Much of the E28 would in fact be carry-over engineering from the E12 it would replace, although many of the less visible elements would be new. It was fortunate for BMW that buyers of medium-sized saloons tended to be somewhat conservative; it allowed them to get away with retaining the door and roof pressings from the previous car, which saved on development and manufacturing costs. The first E28s would also use engines that had made their debut in the E12 range and the same ZF worm-and-roller steering, and most models would also have the same semi-trailing-arm rear suspension. This had a tendency to sudden oversteer, which was tamed for the more powerful E28s by adding a rear anti-roll bar, changing the angle of the trailing arms, and fitting a trailing linkage that picked up where the arms met.

However, engineering pioneered on more recent BMW models would also find its way into the E28s. Notable among

THE E28 M5 (1984–1987)

Very much in the fashion of the 1980s, the E28 models had upright, almost geometric lines. This was a 525i model. BMW

the pioneers was the big E23 7 Series saloon, which had a new double-link front suspension and had also come with a whole range of new electronic gadgetry. This included a service interval indicator, an on-board computer (which calculated such things as journey times and fuel consumption) and automatic cabin temperature regulation. ABS would be a feature of some E28s, and the hydraulic braking circuit was redeveloped with a diagonal split (rather than a front-to-rear split) to suit this. BMW was also able to improve noise suppression and crash deformation management for the E28, and to introduce a neater style of dashboard with an angled centre section that set many secondary controls within the driver's easy reach.

Otherwise, the E28 was clearly a BMW to look at, retaining the forward-leaning 'shark nose' characteristic of the brand at the time, with four headlamps, the inner pair being smaller than the outer. The engines would range from a 1.8-litre 4-cylinder in the 518i to a 3.5-litre 6-cylinder in the 535i. The cars were announced at the Munich Motor Show in 1981, and remained in production for the relatively short period of six years, the last examples being built in December 1987. So the M5 was introduced at roughly the mid-point of the E28 range's production run.

Announcement

The launch of the new medium-sized Mercedes had been just as carefully planned as that of the new BMW super-saloon. Fearing that other new model announcements might be made at the Frankfurt Motor Show in autumn 1984, Mercedes delayed the introduction of their new medium-sized cars. So the new W124 saloon range was announced at a special press event held in Spain towards the end of November, and the first deliveries were scheduled for the early months of 1985.

BMW's plan was to have the first pre-production examples of their new car out on assessment trials by the end of 1984, and those twenty-five cars went out to carefully selected VIP customers from October onwards. Very little is known about them, but they seem to have been numbered within the main sequences reserved for the M5. There was an interesting anomaly here, though. All of these cars (and according to some sources, one more as well) had the standard WBA prefix in their VINs; when volume production began this changed to the WBS prefix that has been associated with the Motorsport division ever since.

It seems clear that these pre-production cars left the Motorsport assembly plant looking as much like the standard 5 Series cars as possible. Disguise would not have been difficult, in any case: specialist tuners such as Alpina already had high-performance derivatives of the E28 range on sale, and some customers asked for these to be de-badged so that their performance potential was not immediately obvious. Therefore anybody who saw a slightly non-standard E28 with an unusual turn of speed before the M5 was announced was likely to think that it was an aftermarket confection of some kind.

THE E28 M5 (1984–1987)

The original plan was to announce the new M5 model to the world at the Geneva Motor Show in March 1985, but it soon became apparent that there was a snag. This was a time when governments in several countries were setting new regulations to reduce exhaust emissions – Germany had already announced some for 1986 – and the Swiss were taking a keen interest in the subject. Development of a 'cleaned-up' M5 with a catalytic converter in the exhaust system had not been high on the priorities list at BMW, and none would be available in time for the Geneva Show. So, reasoning that Swiss sensibilities would be offended by the introduction of a new model without a catalytic converter option at their home show, BMW changed its plans. Instead of being introduced at Geneva, the M5 was introduced at the Amsterdam Show a month earlier.

The pre-production car that appeared at Amsterdam reflected how BMW saw its potential market at the time. As this was to be a hand-built car, the cost would be quite high, and that would limit its potential market to relatively wealthy buyers. These in turn

TOP: **The standard-specification first-generation M5 was a thoroughly discreet machine. Who would have thought that under this sober exterior lurked a 286PS 24-valve engine with motor-sport ancestry?** BMW

BOTTOM: **The front spoiler was deeper than on mainstream E28 models, and of course the grille carried an M5 logo. This picture clearly shows the smaller inner headlamps of the European-model M5.** BMW

■ THE E28 M5 (1984–1987)

Even from behind, there was not much to give away that this was a high-performance saloon. This is the black car pictured on page 25 with number-plate **M-HM 5537**. BMW

A discreet tail spoiler could be added to the boot lid. By the standards of the 1980s it was a quite distinctive 'performance' extra, although it looks quite tame to modern eyes. BMW

THE E28 M5 (1984–1987)

were going to be predominantly in their forties or older, and they were unlikely to want a gaudy confection of the sort that appealed to younger buyers. They were going to want something altogether more subtle – the sort of car that in Britain was known as a 'Q-car' after the disguised 'Q-ships' used on convoy escort duties during the Second World War.

As a result, the M5 that appeared at Amsterdam was different in many ways from the eventual production models. It was very subtle indeed, with standard-looking steel wheels and not a spoiler in sight. However, the feedback assiduously gathered by BMW's marketing department suggested that the car was simply too subtle. So a few modifications were made before M5 production began in earnest, although – as

The optional rear spoiler always had a rubber edge but was otherwise painted to match the bodywork. NICK DIMBLEBY

All M5s had door mirrors painted in the body colour, although on mainstream E28 models they were in matt black plastic. NICK DIMBLEBY

Even the M5 identification could be left off the car if the customer so wished. When fitted, it looked like this, with the Motorsport division's tricolour stripes adorning the M. BMW

Twin tailpipes emerged from under the centre of the rear apron, which, in this case, is the one from the optional bodykit. NICK DIMBLEBY

27

■ THE E28 M5 (1984–1987)

Stylish cross-spoke alloy wheels were another distinguishing feature of the M5. This is the 16-inch size rather than the metric TRX type. NICK DIMBLEBY

if to prove that you cannot please all the people all of the time – some customers went on to ask for the Motorsport tricolour logos that adorned the grille and boot lid to be omitted.

Production cars were given a deeper front air dam that incorporated long-range driving lamps beside the turn indicators. The bottom of this air dam was painted black, and a matching black band was carried through on shallow side skirts to the bottom of the rear wings. Behind the air dam was an aerodynamic undertray for the engine compartment, an item that would always be unique to M5 versions of the E28. The door mirror shells were painted to match the body – subtle indeed, although obvious when seen against a standard E28 with its black plastic mirror bodies. And cross-spoke alloy wheels became part of the specification; these added to the special nature of the M5 by having the metric size demanded by Michelin's new and supposedly more advanced TRX tyres.

CREATING THE E28 M5: THE POWERTRAIN

The Motorsport division's high-performance 3.5-litre M88 engine was, of course, the crucial component around which the E28 M5 came together. The version used for the car was known as an M88/3, being the third iteration of the engine, and had already appeared in the M635 CSi version of the big E24 coupé that went on sale in early 1984 after an autumn 1983 announcement.

Bore and stroke remained unchanged from the original M88 engine, as did the design of the cross-flow cylinder head with its four big valves for each cylinder; the inlet valves had a 37mm diameter and the exhaust valves a 32mm diameter. The 264-degree camshaft was driven by a single roller chain, and the M88/3 engine was developed with conventional wet-sump lubrication, unique pistons and connecting rods, and a Bosch Motronic electronic fuel injection system in place of the Kugelfischer mechanical type used on earlier M88 engines. BMW quoted the maximum power as 286PS at 6,500rpm, with peak torque of 333Nm (245lb ft) at 4,500rpm.

Although this engine left little room around it in the E28's engine bay, it was beautifully presented. The cast alloy valve cover carried the BMW roundel and the legend 'M Power', which both stood out in plain metal against a crackle-black finish. Although the complicated valve train made it rather harsher and more mechanical in sound than other BMW sixes of the time, it was a delightfully smooth engine. Importantly, it was very flexible, too, delivering plenty of low-speed torque that ensured good behaviour in traffic. Notable was that its hunger for space under the bonnet forced the Motorsport engineers to relocate the battery from its standard E28 position to a new one at the right-hand side of the boot, where it also helped to give the car better balance by evening out the weight distribution.

In the M635 CSi, the M88/3 engine had initially been coupled to a five-speed direct-top 'sports' gearbox made by Getrag and featuring a dog's-leg shift gate. However, the unconventional shift gate appears not to have gone down very well with customers, especially in the USA, and so for the M5 a switch was made to an overdrive five-speed type with a conventional shift pattern, and in fact this was also standardized on the M635 CSi during 1985 or early 1986. This gearbox was again made by Getrag, and was their 280/5 model. A feature was pre-loaded gears, which improved the quality of the change. It drove to a 3.73:1 final drive, the same as on the M635 CSi, and this came as standard with a 25 per cent limited-slip differential.

It was this powertrain that made the E28 M5 the fastest production saloon car in the world when it was first launched, with a 0–60mph time of 7.5 seconds that is still quite respectable more than thirty years later, and a maximum speed of 246 km/h (153mph).

THE E28 M5 (1984–1987)

The 286PS engine in the M5 was a development of the M88 type seen in the M1 at the end of the 1970s, and ultimately traced its ancestry back to the M30 'big six'. NICK DIMBLEBY AND BMW

■ THE E28 M5 (1984–1987)

CREATING THE E28 M5: STEERING, SUSPENSION AND BRAKES

If the Motorsport engine was at the heart of the new M5, equally important were the changes that the division's engineers made to the E28 chassis to handle all its extra power and torque.

There were no changes to the fundamental layout of the E28's suspension, which retained MacPherson struts at the front and a semi-trailing arm rear end. However, the ride height was lowered, which demanded some changes to the suspension geometry. The coil springs were stiffer at the front, although initially the rear ones were standard E28 fare. These were matched by monotube gas-filled dampers made by Bilstein. A thicker (21mm) front anti-roll bar was added, as was the 14mm rear anti-roll bar that was standard on the 528i and above, and a rarely specified option for lesser models of the E28. The results were a noticeably firmer ride than in the latter, but a considerable improvement in roll resistance and a generally tauter feel. The quicker steering of the 535i models also helped, with just 3.2 turns lock-to-lock instead of the 3.5 turns on other E28s.

Braking was special. The basics of dual hydraulic circuits and a vacuum servo were retained, and the M5 was drawn up with ABS as standard; on other E28s, the 535i apart, it was at this stage an extra-cost option. The rear discs were unchanged from the 535i models, and were solid types with a 284mm (11.2in) diameter. At the front, however, the M5 went to ventilated discs with the same 284mm diameter and four-piston calipers.

CREATING THE E28 M5: THE INTERIOR

The Motorsport division gave the E28 interior a subtle but effective make-over for the M5. Some elements were changed for practical reasons or out of necessity; others were changed to suit the deliberately sporting nature of the car; and yet others were changed to give the M5 its own special character. It was an irresistible combination that helped set the tone for future cars from the Motorsport division, and it played an important part in the M5's appeal.

Responsible for a major change in the interior ambience was a black headlining, which would always remain unique to M5 derivatives of the E28 range. Next, special seats with the tricolour Motorsport logo on a metal tag attached to their backrests helped to present a distinctive appearance. At the front, these had deep bolsters to improve occupant location, while the rear bench of lesser E28s gave way to two individually moulded seats with an armrest between them. The front seats came with electric adjustment as standard,

All four seats had a neat Motorsport tricolour flash on their backrests. This picture emphasizes the neatness and good taste of the whole car – a characteristic that would become essential to later M5s, too. NICK DIMBLEBY

THE E28 M5 (1984–1987)

The dashboard was remarkably standard for such a car. The steering wheel had a tricolour band on its lower spoke and there is a Motorsport logo on the rev counter, but otherwise non-experts could be forgiven for thinking this was just a well-equipped mainstream E28. BMW

31

■ THE E28 M5 (1984–1987)

TOP LEFT: **BMW's Check Control was still a novelty in the mid-1980s. It was an option on mainstream E28s, but standard on the M5. Even though the buttons on this UK car read in English, the LED read-out above remained in German!** NICK DIMBLEBY

and for those who insisted, Recaro racing bucket seats were made available at extra cost. (Nevertheless, it appears that some cars were specially ordered with the flatter standard E28 seats – perhaps by more corpulent owners.) Upholstery was in Highland cloth or leather, and buffalo hide was made available in a single colour as well. Velour was used for the carpets, the kick-panels on the doors, and the parcel shelf.

The gear selector grip showed not only the gear positions in the five-speed gate, but also displayed a diagonal Motorsport tricolour flash. NICK DIMBLEBY

Clear here is the way the centre of the dashboard was angled towards the driver. This car had leather upholstery, and the switches next to the handbrake grip are for the multi-way electric seat adjustment. BMW

Instruments and controls also came in for attention. The instrument panel gained a unique speedometer that read to 280km/h or 170mph, depending on market requirements, and the rev counter was also special. It had a high 6,900rpm redline with a warning sector from 6,500rpm and carried a discreet Motorsport logo, where the rev counter on other E28s contained an econometer. The steering wheel, adjustable for reach but not for rake, was a three-spoke M-Technic item with a Motorsport tricolour band on its central spoke, and the gearshift grip also carried the M logo. The shift pattern was indicated by a sticker on the face of the ashtray.

Electric windows were already available for the E28 range, and they were standardized for the front doors of the M5; rear-seat passengers had to use manual winders unless the car was ordered with the extra-cost all-round electric windows. Central locking was made standard. While the overhead Check Control panel with its multiple warning lights was standard, an on-board computer system was made an extra-cost option. Inevitably, the selection of 'options' fitted as standard would differ from market to market, but they included air conditioning, front seat heaters, rear head restraints and a powered rear window blind. The ICE (In-Car Entertainment) system installed in the car also varied from country to country, to suit local conditions.

Even the boot interior received special treatment, being lined with plush carpet. The lining under the boot lid was not changed, and on the first cars had the same grey finish as on other E28s; however, it was soon changed on production for a black lining. At about the same time, a special cargo net on the boot floor was added to the original specification.

BUILDING THE FIRST M5S

BMW planned initially to build just 250 M5s every year for world-wide consumption, but the enthusiastic reception that the car received soon made it clear that this would not be enough. All were to be hand-assembled by dedicated teams working for BMW Motorsport, adding the special Motorsport elements to ready-painted E28 bodyshells that were shipped across from the main assembly plant at Dingolfing. The size of the original Motorsport premises at Preussenstrasse in Munich may have had something to do with the cautious annual build plan; the Motorsport division would actually move to new and larger premises at Daimlerstrasse in Garching, some 100km (60 miles) east of Munich, over the summer of 1986.

> ## MICHELIN TRX WHEELS AND TYRES
>
> Tyre manufacturer Michelin introduced its TRX tyre-and-wheel system in 1975, the initial letters picking up the X of the pioneering Michelin radial tyre and the TR standing for 'Tension Répartie' (shared stress).
>
> This was the first time a tyre and wheel had been designed specifically to work together, and its development had been driven by Michelin's search for better roadholding through a lower sidewall height but without a corresponding loss of ride comfort. To achieve what they wanted, Michelin designed tyre and wheel together, using a redesigned wheel rim and tyre bead that gave a very strong bond between tyre and wheel and also gave better stress distribution within the tyre.
>
> The special tyre rim and bead were not compatible with those of conventional wheels and tyres, and so Michelin decided to avoid confusion among users by giving the TRX wheels and tyres metric dimensions instead of the conventional Imperial sizes. Somewhat inevitably, the non-standard dimensions caused problems in the tyre aftermarket and, equally inevitably, rival tyre manufacturers soon developed low-profile tyres with similar advantages that were not only cheaper but fitted on rims with conventional dimensions.
>
> The TRX tyre was no longer fitted as original equipment after a few years, but at the time of writing Michelin continued to make batches of tyres to suit cars that had TRX wheels from new.

Even though the cars were hand-built to order, there was quite a wide 'standard' range of specifications. As the sidebars in this chapter show, for example, there were fourteen standard paint colours from the beginning (the metallics cost extra), along with ten interior options. All these remained available throughout the production run at Preussenstrasse, and most customers were satisfied with them, although a few were keen enough to part with extra cash for some unlisted options.

There were several minor changes to the production specification, too, during this first phase of the M5's life when the cars were still being hand-built at Preussenstrasse. So

■ THE E28 M5 (1984–1987)

from September 1985, power adjustment became available at extra cost for the sports seats, and an M-Technic aero kit with additional spoilers was introduced as an option; this was essentially the kit of spoilers and sills that was standard on the M535i, with distinctive ribbing along the lower edges. In France and Spain, where the additional ostentation it brought met local tastes, the kit became part of the standard specification on 1986 models.

Two more new options became available in November 1985, the major one being a driver's side airbag and the other an uprated ICE system. Different rear springs, unique to the M5, became standard on all models in about March 1986, and several changes arrived together in April. Electric windows all round became standard rather than optional, as did the on-board computer, and the gearshift grip gained an insert showing the shift pattern, together with the Motorsport stripes. At the same time, the label that had originally shown the shift pattern disappeared from the ashtray lid. A new option made available was Shadowline exterior trim, which replaced all the bright metal around the windows, lights and bumpers with matt black items. Then from May 1986, the 16-inch cross-spoke alloy wheels that had already appeared on right-hand-drive cars for Europe became an option in other markets.

The UK was a strong BMW market, and the M5 was made available with right-hand drive to suit. This 1987 car has the optional bodykit of spoiler and sills, although with the black paint it is barely visible without a close look. NICK DIMBLEBY

THE RHD CARS

All the first M5s had been built to the DC91 specification (see box on p.41), which meant that they had left-hand drive and were destined for European markets. However, probably fewer than 400 such cars had been assembled before BMW began production of right-hand-drive models, predominantly for the UK market. These were known as DC92 types, and the first ones were built in March 1986 in Preussenstrasse, although sales did not begin in the UK until July that year.

There had been a few changes to the DC92 cars in addition to the changed position of the steering wheel. The Motorsport engineers had discovered that simply swapping the brake master cylinder and servo to a corresponding position on the right-hand side of the car gave poor braking feel, so these items were repositioned. In those markets destined to receive RHD cars, Michelin had made little headway with its new metric-sized tyres, so BMW decided to use a more conventional 16-inch alloy wheel with a 7.5-inch rim that was made for them by BBS. These took a more readily available size of tyre, and the original tyres fitted were the Pirelli P700 high-performance type. As these were slightly wider than the metric Michelins, cars that had them also had to have small wing extensions to cover them; these were painted to match the body and were as good as invisible.

Cars for the UK market also came as

standard with the electric sunroof that was an extra-cost option in Germany, and their specification included ABS, electric seat adjustment, air conditioning, the on-board computer, electric windows and central locking, heated washer jets, a heated driver's door lock, and a rear window blind.

Just seventy-six right-hand-drive M5 models were built at Preussenstrasse before the plant's summer holiday in 1986. All subsequent examples (111 of them – the final total was 187 cars for the UK) would come from the new Motorsport plant in Garching.

WHAT THE PRESS THOUGHT

Motor Sport, October 1986
(The magazine tested a LHD car that had been registered in the UK.)

'Very pricey indeed in terms of perceived value for money, but as the ultimate upper-crust "Q car", the BMW M5 probably has no peers.'

'Simply shattering performance all the way up the range.'

'At first acquaintance, the M5 seems a little lumpy as you warm it up, but once on the move performs like a turbine, only a shrill – almost metallic – hum betraying the rise in rpm.'

'If you are not very careful getting the M5 off the line energetically, it's possible to induce quite severe axle tramp, so a little bit of finesse is required to coax the best out of this BMW under harsh acceleration.'

'In normal usage it is virtually impossible to induce the M5 to do anything untoward as far as braking adhesion is concerned … You can stand this medium-sized saloon "on its nose" time after exhilarating time with no appreciable diminution of the braking performance.'

'The M5 provides roomy accommodation for four – just the job for the wealthy executive who wants to have a sports car, yet still finds the kids hampering the realisation of that ambition!'

Autosport, 6 November 1986
'If all you want is visual impact, then the M5 is definitely not for you. That sober suit hides pure muscle, the motoring equivalent of Clark Kent hiding Superman.'

'If you're on an autobahn and an errant Porsche holds you up, you can drop down to fourth and zap past him while climbing from 100 to 120mph in 7.6s.'

'One of the beauties of it is that it will waffle along at 1,000rpm or less without a quiver or a shake or a jerk.'

"It isn't what you'd call a quiet engine, but … the noises it makes are spine-tingling."

Car and Driver, December 1987
'A prime example of the high-performance roadware thundering through our times.'

'The M5 is so quick that waiting to pass someone safely creates no frustration: you feel you can afford good traffic manners because the machine quickly compensates for any delays.'

'The M5's insides look like the finely instrumented and tailored pilots' cocoon of a deep-space launch vehicle.'

'You buy this car for its soul.'

'The M5 is outrageously expensive … a no-compromises, foot-to-the-floor screamer built for those who demand the ultimate in speed and refinement. The few who can afford it are going to have a ball.'

■ THE E28 M5 (1984–1987)

ASSEMBLY AT GARCHING

When the Motorsport division moved into its new premises in Garching, new possibilities for the M5 opened up. Even though the E28 models were scheduled to go out of production in 1988 and to be replaced by the E34 5 Series range, there were still two full years to go and BMW planned to exploit the success of the M5 to the full in the time it had left.

So although production of the left-hand-drive DC91 and right-hand-drive DC92 models resumed in the new premises after the summer works holiday, plans were already under way for two more major derivatives to enter production. These became the DC93 (North American) and DC98 (CKD) types.

In the meantime, the cars that began to come from the Garching plant in October 1986 had a small number of differences from their predecessors. There were some new paint colours: Cirrus Blue, Royal Blue and Malachite Green replaced the earlier Arctic Blue, Cosmos Blue and Agate Green, while Polaris metallic disappeared and was not replaced. New 'extended leather' interior options began to appear and were introduced progressively over the next year or so. Otherwise, the only visible change was the introduction of new plates for the door sills, now with an M5 logo. Out of sight were thicker anti-roll bars (25mm at the front and 18mm at the rear) and Boge dampers all round in place of the earlier Bilstein types; the battery cover in the boot changed, too. A further modification, which arrived a few months later in March 1987, was the addition of map-reading lights in the body of the interior mirror.

Cause for celebration: the thousandth BMW M5 was delivered to a couple from Eichenau, near Munich. They are seen here receiving the car from Wolfgang-Peter Flohr, who then headed the Motorsport division. BMW

THE E28 M5 (1984–1987)

THE NORTH AMERICAN CARS

BMW probably never doubted that the M5 would find a ready market in North America, but the special requirements of that market would have created unwelcome production complications at the original Motorsport premises in Preussenstrasse. So the introduction of the North American (and especially, US) versions of the M5 was delayed until production had settled in at Garching. The first examples were built in November 1986.

The most important special feature of the North American M5, or DC93 type, was that it had an emissions-controlled version of the M88 engine. This was developed to use catalytic converters (which would not become obligatory in Europe until after E28 production ended), and was actually given its own type designation to distinguish it from the original European version of the engine. It became an S38 type, or an S38 B35 to give it the full factory code.

The Motorsport division did a fine job of maintaining power and torque in the redeveloped engine, even though the catalytic converters inevitably had a strangling effect. The engine specialists lowered the compression ratio to suit unleaded fuel, and simplified the exhaust manifold shape to give better gas flow; they fitted different camshafts with a 248-degree specification, and added a double-row timing chain. The resulting engine delivered 260PS (256bhp by US standards) and 329Nm (243lb ft) of torque – still big figures by the standards of the day but not quite up to those of the European engine. So to compensate for performance losses, the North American M5s had lower final drive gearing. To distinguish the S38 engine from the M88 original, and perhaps also for marketing reasons associated with North America, the emissions-controlled engine also had a different valve cover with the legend 'BMW M Power' instead of the simple 'M Power' of the M88 type.

The original intention was to build the North American M5 in a limited edition of 500 cars, all of which would be sold as 1988 models beginning in summer 1987. This gave the Motorsport division just a year to produce them, which was quite a tall order for a hand-assembly operation that

The North American versions of the M5 came only in black. Clear here are the extended bumpers with side marker lights, and the four equal-sized headlamps also seen on other North American E28s. The North American cars also came with Shadowline exterior trim as standard: compare the side window frames with those in the picture of a European car on page 34. NICK DIMBLEBY

37

THE E28 M5 (1984–1987)

ABOVE: **This picture shows the third brake light fitted to the North American cars (at the base of the rear window). The tail spoiler was a standard fit for this market.** NICK DIMBLEBY

LEFT: **Most North American cars came with Natur leather upholstery, as seen here.** NICK DIMBLEBY

was also building M5s to European specification in both LHD and RHD forms at the same time. So to simplify the assembly operation, a standard North American specification was devised. The only optional extra that could be added during production was heated front seats.

Like other E28s for North America, the M5s had US-specification impact bumpers with side marker lights in their end caps, and at the front this required a special air dam, which was borrowed from the North American 535i model. Again as on other E28 models sold in the USA, all four headlamps had the same diameter; on European cars, the inner pair had a smaller diameter than the outer pair. All the cars were painted in the same Black, and all of them came with Shadowline blacked-out trim as standard. All had the M-Technic rear spoiler that was an option for the European models. The wheels were universally 16-inch alloys (an obvious choice because the metric tyres were simply not sold in the USA). An electric sunroof was standard, together with electric windows, electrically adjustable front seats, central locking and air conditioning. The interior featured tan ('Natur') leather upholstery, with leather on the door panels and centre console; cruise control and the on-board computer were standard; and there was full carpeting for the boot interior. The standard ICE fit was an AM/FM stereo radio-cassette with eight speakers.

Cars for Canada (of which there were 101) differed slightly, as they had the heated front seats as standard and could be ordered with either Natur or Black leather upholstery; the available figures show that seventy-one cars had the Black leather option. At the very end of North American M5 production, thirty cars for the USA were also built with the Black leather interior. The Canadian cars also had kilometres-per-hour speedometers instead of the miles-per-hour types used in models for the USA.

The North American-specification cars also had a number of suspension differences from the European models. The major difference was the addition of a load-levelling system

THE E28 M5 (1984–1987)

to the rear suspension, which was never made available for any M5 models other than the DC93 types. The front springs and dampers were standard production items, the springs being common to the US-model 535i and the dampers being common to the US-model 635 CSi. The rear springs and 18mm anti-roll bar were shared with the DC91 and DC92 models, and the North American cars had the same 25mm front anti-roll bar as their European contemporaries.

Things did not go quite as smoothly as BMW might have liked for the M5 in North America. For a start, its high fuel consumption made it subject in the USA to the 'gas-guzzler' tax, which was essentially a fine imposed by the government on cars that did not meet a minimum economy figure; this added $2250 to the advertised showroom price. The second problem was that BMW North America had advertised the M5 as a limited edition of 500 examples on its announcement in August 1987; it was then faced with a deluge of orders, which persuaded BMW in Germany to increase that planned total. In all, 1,239 cars would be built for the USA before production ended in November 1987; there were more M5s for North America than for all the model's other markets added together. In 1991, this turned out to be a problem, when litigation-happy American M5 owners banded together and filed a class-action lawsuit against BMW, suing for damages on the grounds that their cars were not as exclusive as they had been led to believe. BMW settled that one in 1993 by giving a $4,000 voucher to each owner; the catch was that it was a voucher against the purchase price or lease of a new BMW!

JAPANESE M5S

BMW also identified a demand in Japan for the M5, and once again created a special derivative to suit the market. Japanese emissions regulations were strict, and so a version of the S38-engined North American model was scheduled for the job. As there was a special prestige in right-hand-drive Japan about owning a left-hand-drive car, the M5s delivered to Japan were in fact variants of the DC93 North American-specification types.

There were just thirty of these cars, all identical and all built between January and March 1987 in Garching. Although they had the same mechanical specification as the North American cars, and the same equal-sized headlamps, they also had a number of unique features. All the cars were finished in Diamond Black metallic with Shadowline trim, and all of them had Highland cloth upholstery in Anthracite, with the usual M logo on the upper backrests. The cars had 16-inch BBS wheels, an electric sunroof and the M-Technic aerodynamic kit. Air conditioning, electric front seats, cruise control, the on-board computer, rear sunblind and velour floor mats were all standard, and the sill plates all carried the M5 logo.

SOUTH AFRICAN M5S

The BMW assembly plant at Rosslyn, near Pretoria in South Africa was opened in 1968 and was the company's first overseas factory. It built cars both for the South African domestic market and for export, and some of them were unique derivatives specially developed to suit local conditions. However, the factory was dependent on major components shipped out from BMW in Germany for local assembly, and by the time of the M5 had nearly 20 years of expertise in assembling cars from CKD kits of parts.

So BMW can have had few misgivings about providing a quantity of M5 models to the Rosslyn factory in CKD form for local sale. There were ninety-six in all, assembled between June 1987 and November 1988 (the latter several months after the last of the E28 5 Series cars had been built in Germany), and they were promoted as a limited edition.

The South African M5s were unique, and were given their own model code of DC98. All had right-hand drive, like the DC92 models, and all had the M88 engine without catalytic converters. They all had the M-Technic bodykit that was an extra-cost option on European cars, with 16-inch wheels and Shadowline blackout trim. There was a limited range of five metallic colours (Cirrus Blue, Delphin Grey, Diamond Black, Henna Red and Ice White) and the South African cars did not have the headlamp wash-wipe system that was standard on German-built cars. An electric sunroof was the only extra-cost option.

There were special features inside these cars, too. They were unique among E28 M5 models in having Nappa leather upholstery as part of a full-leather trim similar to the Highline type available for the E24 6 Series coupés and the big E23 7 Series saloons. So the leather covered not only the seats but also the door panels and upper door trims, the centre console, the dashboard and glovebox lid, the headlining and the sun visors. It came with the usual Motorsport logos on the front and rear seat backrests, and could be

■ THE E28 M5 (1984–1987)

The South African-assembled E28 M5s were yet another variation on the theme. They came with the full bodykit, plus a coachline just above the body side crease. Note, too, the clear reflectors just below the driving lamps, a South African legal requirement. BMW SOUTH AFRICA

PERFORMANCE FIGURES FOR THE E28 M5 MODELS

European saloon	0–60mph	6.2 sec
	Maximum	246km/h (153mph)
US-spec saloon	0–60mph	6.5 sec
	Maximum	238km/h (148mph)

Note that some road tests achieved even better times and speeds.

had in a choice of four colours (Indigo, Lotus White, Mid-silver and Natur). Despite this generally high level of trim, the DC98 cars nevertheless had some deletions from the European specification. There was no storage tray on the passenger's side of the dashboard, only the front door sill plates carried the M5 logo, and the black boot-lid liner was omitted even though the boot was otherwise fully carpeted in the usual way.

PRODUCTION TOTALS FOR THE E28 M5

Just 2,241 examples of the E28 M5 were built between October 1984 and November 1988 (although production in Germany ceased in December 1987, the South African cars were assembled there in 1988). Figures gathered by Thomas G. Müller for his monumental book, *Die Grosse BMW M Chronik*, show the following.

Type	Build dates	Total
DC91	October 1984–September 1985	195
	September 1985–September 1986	337
	September 1986–September 1987	54
	September 1987	2
	(Sub-total)	**588**
DC92	March 1986–July 1986	76
	September 1986–September 1987	105
	September 1987–October 1987	6
	(Sub-total)	**187**
DC93	November 1986–September 1987	740
	September 1987–October 1987	260
	October 1987–June 1988	370
	(Sub-total)	**1,370**
DC98	June 1987–November 1988	96
	(Sub-total)	**96**
	Grand total	**2,241**

Notes:
(1) DC91 cars were European-specification LHD types
DC92 cars were European-specification RHD types (mainly for UK)
DC93 cars were North American-specification LHD types; they include 30 cars for Japan (see main text)
DC98 cars were CKD types assembled in South Africa.
(2) The Japanese DC93 cars were built from January to March 1987.
(3) There were 1,370 DC93 cars, but only 1,340 for North America (USA and Canada); the other 30 were the cars for Japan.
(4) The South African cars left Germany in kit form between March and June 1987, but were built up at Rosslyn between June 1987 and November 1988.

Annual production by model-year

Year	Period		
1985	(October 1984–September 1985)	195 DC91	195
1986	(October 1985–September 1986)	337 DC91	
		76 DC92	413
1987	(October 1986–September 1987)	56 DC91	
		105 DC92	
		740 DC93	
		96 DC98	997
1988	(October 1987–June 1988)	6 DC92	
		630 DC93	636
	Grand total		**2,241**

■ THE E28 M5 (1984–1987)

PAINT AND UPHOLSTERY OPTIONS

October 1984 to August 1986

There were fourteen paint colours available in this period. Names are shown in their English forms.

Colour	Code	Colour	Code
Agate Green metallic	177	Cosmos Blue metallic	185
Alpine White	146	Diamond Black metallic	181
Arctic Blue metallic	045	Delphin metallic	184
Black	086	Lapis Blue	173
Bronzit metallic	139	Polaris metallic	060
Burgundy Red metallic	199	Sable Brown metallic	196
Cinnabar Red	138	Salmon Silver metallic	203

There were five Highland cloth upholstery options in this period:

Colour	Code	Colour	Code
Anthracite	0186/0257	Pearl Beige	0189
Nutria	0188	Pine Green	0190
Pacific Blue	0187		

These were accompanied by five leather options; note that Anthracite was Buffalo leather:

Colour	Code	Colour	Code
Anthracite	0180	Pacific Blue	0204
Black	0203	Pearl Beige	0206/0287
Cardinal Red	0256/0289		

September 1986 to November 1987

There were thirteen paint colours available in this period. Names are shown in their English forms.

Colour	Code	Colour	Code
Alpine White	146	Diamond Black metallic	181
Black	086	Lapis Blue	173
Bronzit metallic	139	Malachite Green metallic	205
Burgundy Red metallic	199	Royal Blue metallic	198
Cinnabar Red	138	Sable Brown metallic	196
Cirrus Blue metallic	189	Salmon Silver metallic	203
Delphin metallic	184		

THE E28 M5 (1984–1987)

The cloth and leather upholstery options were the same as before, but five more 'extended leather' types were progressively added to the list to give a total of fifteen upholstery choices:

Colour	Code	Colour	Code
Anthracite	0284	Natur	0237
Black	0232	Silver	0233
Cardinal Red	0239		

Note that Black, Natur and Silver were theoretically available from June 1986; Cardinal Red from September 1986; and Anthracite arrived only towards the end of production in September 1987.

Japan
There was only ever one paint option for Japanese cars. This was Diamond Black metallic, which had colour code 181. All Japanese E28 M5s came with Anthracite Highland cloth (0186/0257) interior trim.

North America (USA and Canada)
There was only ever one paint option for North American cars. This was Black, which had colour code 086.
In the USA, the standard interior was in Natur extended leather (0237), but thirty cars were built at the end of production with Black extended leather (0232). Both options were offered throughout the E28 M5's availability in Canada.

South Africa
There were five paint options on cars assembled in South Africa, of which two were unique to them.

Colour	Code	Colour	Code
Cirrus Blue metallic	189	Henna Red	413
Delphin metallic	184	Ice White	346
Diamond Black metallic	181		

The South African cars also had their own set of interior trim options. All four of these had the 'Highline' style seen on other BMW models.

Colour	Code	Colour	Code
Indigo	N/K	Midsilver	N/K
Lotus White	N/K	Natur	N/K

■ THE E28 M5 (1984–1987)

E28 M5 SPECIFICATIONS

Engines:

Non-catalyst models (DC91, DC92 and DC98)

Type M88/3 6-cylinder petrol
3453cc (93.4mm x 84mm)
Twin overhead camshafts, chain-driven
Four valves per cylinder
Seven-bearing crankshaft
Compression ratio 10.5:1
Bosch Motronic electronic fuel injection
286PS (282bhp) at 6,500rpm
333Nm (245lb ft) at 4,500rpm

Catalyst models (DC93)

Type S38 B35 6-cylinder petrol
3453cc (93.4mm x 84mm)
Twin overhead camshafts, chain-driven (duplex chain)
Four valves per cylinder
Seven-bearing crankshaft
Compression ratio 9.8:1
Bosch Motronic electronic fuel injection
260PS (256bhp) at 6,500rpm
329Nm (243lb ft) at 4,500rpm

Transmission:
Five-speed Getrag 280/5 manual gearbox
Ratios 3.51:1, 2.08:1, 1.35:1, 1.00:1, 0.81:1

Axle ratio:
3.73:1 with non-catalyst engines
3.91:1 with catalyst-equipped engines
(25 per cent limited-slip differential standard on all models)

Suspension, steering and brakes:
Front suspension with MacPherson struts, coil springs, Bilstein (later Boge) gas dampers and 21mm (later 25mm) anti-roll bar
Rear suspension with semi-trailing arms, coil spring struts, Bilstein (later Boge) gas dampers and 18mm anti-roll bar
ZF recirculating-ball steering with 15.1:1 ratio and standard power assistance
Disc brakes all round, 284mm (11.2in) ventilated on front wheels and 284mm (11.2in) solid on rear wheels; twin hydraulic circuits; ABS standard

Dimensions:
Overall length:	4,620mm (181.9in)
	4,800mm (189.0in) (with US bumpers)
Overall width:	1,699mm (66.9in)
Overall height:	1,415mm (55.7in)
Wheelbase:	2,624mm (103.3in)

Wheels and tyres:
185TR390 (metric) five-stud alloy wheels with 220/55VR390 TRX tyres, or
7.5J x 16 five-stud alloy wheels on 225/50VR16 tyres

Kerb weights:
European spec	1,430kg/3,153lb
US spec	1,550kg/3,417lb

CHAPTER THREE

THE 3.6-LITRE E34 M5

The first-generation M5 had certainly started something, and it had caught other manufacturers by surprise. Real high-performance saloons had tended to be very expensive purpose-built machines, and the idea that they could be built on the same platform as an everyday family saloon and still find a willing audience seemed not to have occurred to other car makers, who now scrambled to develop models that would compete for this new market.

It took time, though. Not until 1990 did Mercedes-Benz and the European arm of General Motors release their contenders. From GM came the Lotus-developed Vauxhall Carlton (Opel Omega in some countries) with its outrageous 283km/h (176mph) maximum speed, and from Mercedes came the 500E, 'responsibly' limited to 257km/h (160mph) but certainly capable of more with the limiter removed.

Anticipating that this might happen, BMW had included the preparation of a second-generation M5 model in their schedule for the new 5 Series, the E34 range that was launched in January 1988. BMW Motorsport had meanwhile been closely involved in the development of this, with the result that it was able to field an M5 derivative as early as August 1988. As had been the case with the car it replaced, the new one was visually understated, and to most people it looked like just another E34 5 Series. There was very much more to it than its appearance suggested, however.

THE E34 5 SERIES

Not surprisingly, the E34 5 Series models had some very close similarities to the acclaimed E32 7 Series, the big BMW saloon range that had been introduced two years earlier. In the UK, *Motor* magazine headed its report on the new cars 'Son of Seven', and it was certainly true that the cars looked a lot like their bigger sisters.

The E34 saloon was an exceptionally good-looking car, and arguably more attractive than its 124-series rival from Mercedes-Benz. This is an early UK model from the mainstream range. BMW

45

■ THE 3.6-LITRE E34 M5

The rather angular look that had characterized the E28s had been swept away in favour of the more rounded, aerodynamic shape pioneered on the E32s. Scaled down for the medium-sized saloons, it still worked extremely well, and it gave them a presence that the earlier 5 Series cars had lacked. Yet these were not small cars by any means, and were actually 100mm (3.9in) longer and 51mm (2in) wider than the E28s they replaced. More important perhaps was a fundamental change in proportions, which brought a wheelbase that was 136mm (5.35in) longer than before. This put the wheels nearer the corners of the car to improve ride comfort and also allowed extra length in the passenger compartment. The E34s were only 3mm (0.1in) lower than the E28s, but the extra length and sleek styling made them look much more streamlined and aerodynamic.

The extra width allowed for more passenger space and of course for wider wheel tracks to improve stability as well. Though it also created a larger front area for the car, the more tapered overall profile with its low nose and high tail ensured that BMW was able to claim a Cd of between 0.30 and 0.32 for the earliest E34 models. This was up to 50 per cent better than on the E28s. Detail design played its part here, naturally; not only were the windscreen and rear window more steeply raked, but the windscreen and side windows were less inset than before (BMW had learned something from Audi's experiment with flush glazing here). Spoilers were subtly integrated into the body shape, too. The small front air dam was barely noticeable, and the shaped trailing edge to the boot lid looked more like a concession to style than to the science of aerodynamics that had created it.

Computer-aided design had enabled BMW to make the new bodyshell considerably stiffer than its predecessor, with an increase of just 5 per cent in weight for the bare shell. Stiffened joints at all major body junctions, stronger sills and bonded front and rear screens all made their contribution. The central passenger cell was also capable of remaining largely intact in a 35mph barrier crash, which was 5mph above the contemporary requirement.

Very important for the car's looks was that the latest US regulations now stipulated resistance to a 2.5mph collision, and not the 5mph collision that had required the ugly impact bumpers needed on earlier cars. So BMW was able to integrate the US-mandated collision-resistant bumpers

The E34 M5 had a very well-balanced shape, which was certainly enhanced by the bigger wheels and lower ride height of the car. BMW

THE 3.6-LITRE E34 M5

The E34 M5 looked particularly good in dark colours, which suited the car's essential understatement. M5 badges and spoilers, a lowered ride height and special wheels are really the only clues that these two cars are not just mainstream E34 models. BMW

■ THE 3.6-LITRE E34 M5

into the basic design and, to save cost and complication in production, it standardized these for all markets.

All models had green-tinted heat-filtering glass with the radio aerial incorporated in the rear screen demister element. Inside the cabin, a more rounded facia incorporated a new heater with separate rotary controls for the left and right sides of the car, plus automatic temperature regulation. Air conditioning – automatic again – was an extra-cost option, but the latest version of the Electronic Check Control system was now standard. The rear seats always had a three-point inertia-reel belt for the centre passenger, and special attention had been paid to sound insulation and to door seals, to ensure that the E34s were remarkably quiet cars. Special care had been taken in designing the electrical circuits, which now had high-quality connectors; BMW had learned a lot since their first 7 Series cars in the late 1970s had earned an unenviable reputation for electrical unreliability. Headlamps had a new ellipsoid design that gave superb lighting with excellent beam control.

IN THE BEGINNING

The mainstream E34 models had been on sale for about two months when BMW announced the new M5 model in August 1988. Quite clearly, it had been developed alongside the mainstream models rather than tacked on to the range as an afterthought, which had been the case with the E28 M5s.

However, the new M5 was not in any sense a volume-produced model. Although the bodies were pressed out and assembled at the main factory in Dingolfing that also built bodies for the mainstream E34s, they were then sent to the BMW Motorsport plant in Garching, where they were completed by hand with the special Motorsport powertrains and interior trim. Each car was generally assembled either by one man or by a small team of specialists, and the normal build time was about two weeks.

Much of the original M5's appeal had been in its understated appearance, and the same approach was used for the

One thing had not changed from the previous model, and that was the M5 badge. NICK DIMBLEBY

Subtle technology: the M5's special M System wheels had a distinctive design that concealed their multi-part construction. The heart of the wheel was a five-spoke alloy, and the outer sections were designed to get more cooling air to the brakes. NICK DIMBLEBY AND BMW

48

E34 model, so the front spoiler extension, rear apron and side skirts were all blacked out and barely visible from a distance. The front spoiler also had an extra pair of cooling slots for the radiator and the oil cooler. There was no rear spoiler, although a body-colour item became available as an extra-cost option in November 1988. All this did help with the aerodynamics, although the drag coefficient was not spectacular, ending up at the same 0.32 as for the 535i model.

Shadowline exterior trim (where the bright metal highlights were finished in satin black) was available at extra cost, and all cars came with a black plastic panel between the rear light clusters and with polished twin exhaust tailpipes. An electric sunroof was made optional, along with heated washer jets for the headlamps. But perhaps the most readily recognizable feature of the first E34 M5s was a new style of road wheel. Known as the M System type (and later as M System I), this had a 17-inch diameter and a multi-part design that had been developed and patented by BMW.

The visible element was a pressure-cast magnesium cover with a turbine design, developed in a wind tunnel. The magnesium covers were handed, and radial fins behind them directed cold air onto the brake discs for better stopping power at high speeds. The load-bearing wheels behind were black five-spoke alloys with an asymmetric rim hump that helped retain the tyre after a puncture. The standard wheels had 8J rims, and a 9J rim with wider tyres was made available at extra cost for fitting to the rear wheels to give slicker handling. Factory-fit tyres were by Pirelli or Michelin. These special wheels would never be made available on other versions of the E34.

THE E34 M5's POWERTRAIN

There was still plenty of life left in the Motorsport division's 24-valve 6-cylinder engine, although there was never any doubt that its capacity should be increased for the E34 M5 engine. Lengthening the stroke by 2mm gave a swept volume of 3535cc, which made the S38 B36 engine the largest 6-cylinder type BMW had ever made up to that time. Strictly speaking, that capacity would have merited a 3.5-litre designation, but it was important to make clear that this engine was different from the 3430cc 3.5-litre available in the 535i models, so it was always called a 3.6-litre.

Under the bonnet was once again the 24-valve 6-cylinder Motorsport engine, now delivering 315PS. BMW

■ THE 3.6-LITRE E34 M5

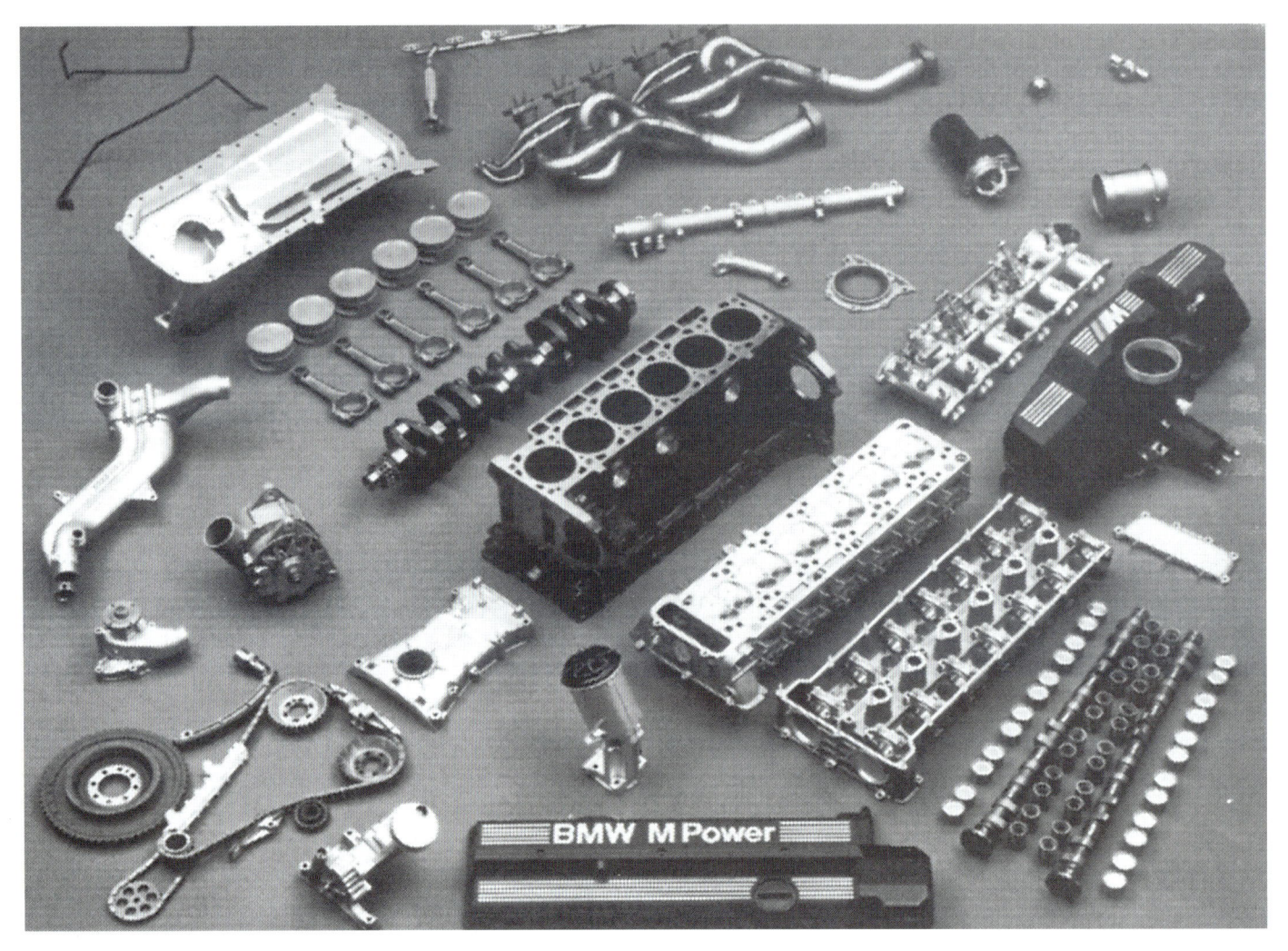

BMW liked to show the component parts of its engines, and these belong to the 3.6-litre type in an E34 M5. They make a persuasive case for most owners to leave work on such an engine to an expert! BMW

Most countries were going to want the engine with a catalytic converter, and it was designed to take one as standard. However, not every country received the same engine. Those for Europe and most other countries had three-way ceramic catalysts and 315PS, but cars for North America and Switzerland had a different exhaust catalyst and 311PS. There were even versions without a catalytic converter for the Gulf States and South Africa, and for those the power output was quoted as 318PS.

The long stroke was achieved with a new forged steel crankshaft, and the compression ratio was raised to 10:1. The camshafts and valve timing were new for this engine, and a variable-length inlet manifold with racing-inspired electronic butterfly valve was added to help improve torque. The intake system was also new, and now featured a hot-wire air mass metering system and a separate throttle for each cylinder. As before, there were equal-length stainless-steel exhaust manifolds. Bosch Motronic engine management was employed once again, and there was a different flywheel.

There was no reason to change from the Getrag 280/5 overdrive five-speed gearbox that had been used in the E28 M5, so this was used again behind the new engine, with the same ratios as before. The final drive was settled at 3.91:1 – the same as on the catalyst versions of the E28 – and, again as before, a 25 per cent limited-slip differential was standardized.

THE 3.6-LITRE E34 M5

THE E34 M5's STEERING, SUSPENSION AND BRAKES

The basic suspension layout of the E34 was adopted unchanged for the M5, although the body was set to ride 20mm lower than a 535i and the spring rates were 25 per cent higher. The dampers had stiffer valves and there were fatter anti-roll bars, up to 25mm from the standard 23mm at the front, and to 18mm from the standard 15mm at the rear. At the rear end, a self-levelling system was added to prevent loads from affecting the handling. There was adjustable toe-in, and 'elasto-kinematics' aided wheel control, with bushes compliant enough to allow the whole axle to toe in during cornering and so generate safe understeer. Wider rear wheels and tyres were made available as an extra-cost option to improve grip in hard cornering.

The standard ABS braking system served ventilated front discs that were thicker and larger in diameter than those on any other E34 model. Steering was essentially the same as on standard E34s, but with a quicker 15.6:1 ratio instead of their 16.2:1. On the M5, it also came as standard with a power assistance system that was dependent on engine speed for the amount of assistance it provided. At extra cost, the Motorsport division also offered a new Servotronic system made by ZF, which varied the amount of assistance

The 3.6-litre engine is seen here both in and out of the car. It was a further development of the M88 engine seen in the E28 M5 and latterly recoded S38.
BMW

Anatomie eines Souveräns.

M5: 232kW/315PS. Beschleunigung von 0-100 km/h in 6,3 s. Höchstgeschwindigkeit 250 km/h*.
*Abgeregelt

BMW issued this interesting drawing when the cars were new. It is headed 'Anatomy of a Sovereign', and below the picture is a reminder that this version of the M5 had 315PS (or 232kW), reached 100km/h from rest in 6.3 seconds and had a governed maximum speed of 250km/h. BMW

to suit the vehicle's road speed. This was later standardized on some models for some countries, as noted below.

THE E34 M5's INTERIOR

As they had done for the E28 models, the Motorsport division based the interior design of the new M5 on that used in the standard E34 models. The changes began with door sill plates bearing the M5 logo, and the boot was fully carpeted in wool with a special stowage compartment on the left-hand side. A leather lining was an extra-cost option.

The steering wheel was a unique three-spoke M-Technic II type with moulded thumb grips and a Motorsport logo on the third spoke. This wheel did not incorporate an airbag. The dials on the instrument panel had red needles, and an oil temperature gauge replaced the economy gauge of other E34s. There was an M logo between the unique 300km/h (186mph) speedometer and rev-counter dials. The instruments also included an integrated Check Control vehicle monitoring system, and a very special touch was a leather-covered M-Technic gearshift grip bearing the tricolour Motorsport stripe and featuring an illuminated shift pattern. A car telephone and twelve-speaker ICE system were additional options.

As for the seats, the E34 M5s came with the sports front seats that were the same as the optional type for other E34 models – although different upholstery gave them a unique appearance. Electric adjustment was available, but was not standardized for all countries, and a position memory was a further option. The rear seats were arranged as individual sports types, with a centre stowage console between them that ensured these cars would be four-seaters. For extra

THE 3.6-LITRE E34 M5

TOP RIGHT: **The architecture of the dashboard was unchanged from the mainstream cars, of course, but note the subtle touches here that distinguish it as belonging to an M5. There are M logos between the main instrument dials and on the steering wheel's lower spoke, and a tricolour flash on the gearshift grip.** BMW

BELOW RIGHT: **All the early cars came with a rear console that made them strictly four-seater saloons.** BMW

BELOW LEFT: **Subtle changes accompanied different specifications: note how the M logo has changed positions on this car.** BMW

cost, electric adjustment of each individual seat was available. Rear head restraints were standard, and for further extra cost these could be linked to the colour-coded seat belts so that they lowered out of sight when the belts were not in use by passengers. This feature was probably introduced as a deliberate tilt at Mercedes in the specification stakes, as the latest Mercedes 124-series saloons and coupés had rear head restraints that could be dropped out of sight to improve rearward visibility – but the Mercedes system had to be operated by the driver.

Both cloth and leather upholstery options were available on the E34 M5s, the check cloth being unique to the M5 and known (unsurprisingly) as M cloth. It came with leather bolsters as standard. The headlining was normally leather with both types of upholstery. The leather upholstery came in three styles, but always used Nappa leather. The basic version used leather only for the seat facings; next up was 'extended leather', which featured leather on the centre console, glovebox lid and door pulls; and above that came 'complete leather', which added leather to the top of the dashboard, the windscreen pillars, the sun visors, the upper door panels and the rear parcels shelf. With this type of interior trim, the headlining was always changed to one made of Alcantara. Actual availability of the different types varied from country to country.

In practice, some cars were built to special order with custom-finished interiors under the BMW Individual scheme. There were cars with custom upholstery and trim styles, and with special ICE systems, carphone fits, fax machines and even TV sets. As Germany's aftermarket custom-building specialists were prepared to meet one-off requests, so BMW had to be, too.

■ THE 3.6-LITRE E34 M5

TOP: **These are the leather seats in an E34 M5, with the electric adjustment controls clearly visible. Note the colourless M5 logo on the sill plate.** BMW

BOTTOM: **The rear seats in this early car are divided by the centre console. A justifiable criticism of the E34 models was a lack of legroom for rear-seat passengers.** BMW

PRODUCTION CHANGES FOR THE 3.6-LITRE E34 M5

The original 3.6-litre version of the E34 M5 was in production between April 1988 and April 1993, although from the end of 1991 it was replaced in most countries by a further-developed car with a 3.8-litre engine. Those cars are the subject of Chapter 4.

There were relatively few production changes in those five years. An early one occurred in October 1989, when the solid rear brake discs were changed for ventilated discs of the same diameter. The main changes were introduced all together in September 1990 on the 1991 models. None of them was major, but the most noticeable was inside the passenger cabin, where the console between the rear seats was deleted and a bench rear seat became standard. The console and individual rear seats nevertheless remained available to special order at extra cost in many countries. At the same time, velour boot trim replaced the standard wool type (leather remained an extra-cost option), and the boot was given a storage box on each side and a luggage net on the floor.

THE RHD CARS

The vast majority of E34 M5s were built with left-hand drive, to the HD91 (European) or HD93 (North American) specifications. Nevertheless, there was significant demand from right-hand-drive countries, primarily Britain, for the high-

THE 3.6-LITRE E34 M5

performance BMW. So a right-hand-drive (HD92) specification was drawn up and production began in December 1989.

Between then and the end of HD92 production in November 1991, either 524 or 531 right-hand-drive cars were built, the precise figure being disputed by different sources. These HD92 models were the first variety of E34 M5 to cease production.

A total of 200 cars was initially scheduled for the UK, where the E34 M5 was announced at the London Motorfair in October 1989. The first examples reached showrooms in February 1990. Other countries that took right-hand-drive M5s included Australia and some Middle Eastern states.

There were also right-hand-drive cars for South Africa, but these were built in-territory and there is more about them below. They had a separate build code of HD98 and were counted separately from the HD92 models.

THE NORTH AMERICAN CARS

The story of the North American-specification E34 M5 is much more complicated than it appears at first sight. There were four distinct stages of production, which began in December 1989, September 1990, July 1991 and September

---

WHAT THE PRESS THOUGHT

Fast Lane, May 1990

'This car could easily be capable of more than 160mph.'

'The engine needs to be worked ... [and] nothing much happens until the rev counter is showing nearly 4000 ... you do always need to be ready to drop two gears in order to blast past a queue.'

'No series production car of similar size can match the BMW for standing start acceleration, or even come close with such a minimum of fuss. The M series engine's extraordinary working range is a matter of wonderment at all times, not least because the usual grit-your-teeth area between six and 7,000rpm can be transcended with no sensation of fear for the reciprocating bits beneath the bonnet.'

'The gear-change is light, if slightly rubbery, while the clutch is heavy, and this particular combination sometimes makes smooth driving a matter of concentration.'

'Either side of the straight ahead the steering is rather dead ... [but it] improves dramatically when you start to press on.'

'On more than one occasion while threading along wet country lanes, the car would understeer quite dramatically without any real provocation.'

'The feel of the middle pedal ... is awful. There's too much servo assistance.'

Road & Track, August 1990

'The M5 has that rare quality of being not only fast, but also able to accelerate to high speeds with absolutely no drama. In fact, it can be so quiet and smooth that you can hardly believe the speedometer.'

'Subjectively, the M5 is remarkably well balanced, with agile handling and rewarding steering feel.'

Car South Africa, June 1991

'A really impressive car which sets new sports sedan standards in terms of performance, ride, road-holding and comfort. Not a car for those who are not keen on driver involvement, but certainly one for the enthusiast who knows what he wants and can afford the price of what is, in all likelihood, the best sports sedan in the world.'

THE 3.6-LITRE E34 M5

There were minimal differences between the European and North American cars. Only the side marker lights in the bumper wraparounds mark this out as a North American model – although it also lacks the side repeater indicators fitted to many of the European cars. NICK DIMBLEBY

1992, respectively. In addition, there was a special Canadian specification that was applied to 194 (about 11.6 per cent) of the HD93 or North American-specification cars. All these cars were visually unchanged from the European models, except for the side marker lights in their front and rear bumper wraparounds. They also came as standard with BMW's four-spoke airbag steering wheel.

The cars were introduced to North America in 1990, nearly three years after the last of the North American E28 M5s had been built. Production actually began as early as December 1989 to build up launch stocks, and although all North American M5s were titled as 1991 models, the first 508 had what could be called a 1990 specification.

The 'true' 1991 models began to leave the assembly lines in Germany in September 1990, and they incorporated a number of changes from the earlier cars. Most noticeable was a change from ellipsoid headlights and fog lights to 'free form' types. Inside the passenger cabin, a tilt-adjustable steering column was added, the radio head unit was changed for a newer type, and the rear console on the earlier cars was deleted. There was a change to the upholstery options, too, as Light Silver Gray Nappa leather (0438) replaced the original Silver Gray Nappa leather (0227). Six months into production, there were further changes, as Calypso Red (252) and Mauritius Blue (287) metallic paints were added to the options list in March 1991. All these cars had 8-inch wheel rims; the 9-inch option for the rear wheels of European cars was never made available on the HD93 models.

The third stage of North American M5 production began in July 1991, when the first of the 1992-model cars were built. The biggest change at this stage was to a taller 3.73:1 final drive that gave better fuel economy (European cars did not follow suit, but retained the original 3.91:1 ratio). ZF Servotronic power-assisted steering, which adjusted the degree of assistance to suit the road speed, replaced the earlier type that varied its assistance according to engine speed on models for the USA (but not, it seems, for Canada), and the clutch was lightened. Remote central locking now became standard and so did a diversity radio antenna, embedded in the rear window glass. There was then a further mid-season change, when the 3.8-litre style of door sill plates with its more prominent M5 logo was used from March 1992.

The fourth and final stage of the North American M5's production was possibly the most interesting, because from September 1992 the cars took on the cosmetic features of the latest European 3.8-litre M5s but retained their 3.6-litre engines. On the outside, the grey lower panel option switched to lighter Granite Silver metallic, there were M System II ('throwing star') wheels, M-Technic aerodynamic door mirrors, and front door handles carrying the BMW Motorsport name. Inside the cabin, the rim of the four-spoke steering wheel now had tricolour stitching, and the wood trim was in grey or black bird's-eye maple. There were some new paint colours, too, and from car number BK06442 Shadowline exterior trim became standard.

The cars sold in Canada were different again, and were immediately recognizable by the standard headlight washers that were not available in the USA. All the other differences lay inside the passenger cabin, where there was a km/h speedometer and the driver's side airbag and knee bolster were only an optional fitment instead of standard as in the USA. Power-assisted steering-column adjustment was never available (it was optional on 1992 cars for the USA), and nor was the Servotronic power steering optional on 1992 and 1993 models in the USA.

Heated front seats were standard (though optional in the USA) and a driver's seat position memory was optional on both 1992 and 1993 models (it was an option for 1992 only in the USA). The rear console standard on cars built before September 1990 became optional thereafter, although it was no longer available on US cars. A ski bag was also standard equipment, although not available in the USA.

As an alternative to the standard Nappa leather upholstery, Canadian cars could be had with 'extended' leather, where leather was used to trim the centre console, the glovebox lid and the door pulls. This again was not available on US cars. (However, the bird's-eye maple trim optional on 1993 cars could not be had with the extended-leather upholstery.)

The 1993 model-year was the last one for North American M5s, although the European-specification cars remained in production as 3.8-litre models for a further two years. One of the last North American-specification cars was presented to the State Police in South Carolina, where BMW was by then building its first US factory at Spartanburg for a 1994 opening.

NORTH AMERICAN M5 PRODUCTION

There were 1,678 E34 M5s built with the North American specification between 1989 and 1993. The build figures for each model-year were as follows:

Year	Units	Note
1990	508	(These were built as 1991 models)
1991	788	
1992	121	
1993	261	

Of the 1,678 North American cars, 194 were built with the Canadian specification that is described in the text. There were therefore 1,484 cars for the USA.

JAPANESE AND MIDDLE EAST MODELS

It appears that some of the late 3.6-litre North American-specification cars were delivered to customers in Japan and the Middle East after 3.8-litre E34 production had started.

SOUTH AFRICAN M5S

The E28 models built in South Africa for the local market had been a sales success, and it was no surprise that BMW decided to send a quantity of E34 models out in CKD form for assembly at the Rosslyn plant. As before, these were given their own distinctive model code, in this case HD98, and were of course right-hand-drive types.

This time, a far greater number of cars went out to Rosslyn, which was also assembling other E34s for local sale. The first CKD kits left Germany in June 1990 and the first cars went on sale in September, three months later. The last kits were shipped out at the end of 1992 and were built up in March 1993.

The South African cars did not differ significantly from German-built right-hand-drive HD92 models, although the ZF Servotronic power steering option was not available. All the South African cars had 'extended' Nappa leather upholstery with leather door panel inserts that were not found elsewhere. They had a generally high level of standard equipment, and were available in a range of colours that suited those in use at the Rosslyn plant. These included white, black, silver and a dark red metallic. South African appreciation of the car was well summed up by *Car* magazine for June 1991, which noted in its test that the M5 was 'not a car for those who are not keen on driver involvement, but certainly one for the enthusiast who knows what he wants and can afford the price of what is, in all likelihood, the best sports sedan in the world'.

THE E35 M5 CONVERTIBLE

Although no convertible version of the E34 5 Series ever entered production, a convertible derivative was certainly developed, and according to some sources it was given the project code of E35. How many prototypes were actually built is not clear, but one was built up with an M5 specification.

■ THE 3.6-LITRE E34 M5

The M5 convertible certainly looked good, but something would have to be done about that underbody strengthening before it was ready for production. DAVE SMITH

BMW have never confirmed the story that this car was built as yet another 'spoiler' in the company's rivalry with Mercedes-Benz. That story says that Mercedes were planning to introduce a convertible version of their 124-series coupé at the Geneva Show in March 1989. In reality, they did not, and their convertible did not appear until 1991. Nevertheless, BMW had supposedly learned of the original plan, and decided to counter it by showing a concept M5 convertible. The Mercedes, had it appeared, would probably have had that company's latest 24-valve 3-litre engine with 220PS, so showing a 315PS M5 convertible would certainly have scored a point for BMW.

In any case, the BMW M5 convertible concept car was the brainchild of Karl-Heinz Kalbfell, who was in charge of the Motorsport division in 1988. Its build was overseen by Thomas Ammerschläger, who would later become director of engineering and production at BMW M, and the car was supposedly built for Gerhard Richter, a senior figure in the Motorsport division who would later join its management board.

The base vehicle was a 540i, which had its roof removed and was turned into a two-door car with a windscreen more steeply raked than the E34 saloon type. The bodyshell was reinforced with massive metal strengthening bars under the sills, and these were still visible when the project was brought to a halt. No doubt a neater solution would have been found for a production car. With its electrically operated convertible top, the car ended up weighing over 100kg (220 lb) more than an M5 saloon. Front seats with integral safety belts were taken from the contemporary E31 8 Series coupés, the passenger cabin was upholstered in leather, and the car was painted Daytona Violet – a colour not yet available on standard-production M5s.

The car still exists in the BMW M historic collection in Munich, and was shown to the media in 2010 as part of the celebrations surrounding the twenty-fifth anniversary of the M5. By that stage it had been fitted with the M System II 'throwing star' wheels and had the Granite Silver lower body paint associated with the 3.8-litre E34 M5s that did not enter production until 1991.

So why did the convertible E34 go no further? There were probably several reasons, and among them is the possibility that it was never intended seriously as a production model but was only meant to upstage Mercedes-Benz at that 1989 Geneva Show. BMW has consistently said as little as possible about it.

SPECIAL EDITIONS OF THE 3.6-LITRE E34 M5

BMW had experimented with special editions in its Motorsport range as early as 1988, when it introduced a Europameister 88 Celebration Edition of the M3 in honour of the racing M3's domination of Group A racing that year. The M5 was not, of course, a track weapon like the M3, but there was no reason not to try a similar marketing ploy with the larger saloon.

So two of the BMW racing drivers were (supposedly, at least) asked to put forward a specification for their ideal M5 in 1991, and limited-edition models based on these suggestions were put on sale in spring 1991. It was a clever way of generating showroom traffic in advance of the 3.6-litre M5's replacement by the 3.8-litre model. The two drivers involved were Johnny Cecotto and Joachim Winkelhock, and their specifications – rather conveniently, perhaps – produced two very different takes on the M5 theme. Cars of both editions also came with a special leather service book pouch, a branded key holder and a gold pin.

The Cecotto Edition

The Cecotto Edition was of twenty cars, although in fact twenty-two were built in all because there were two pre-production examples. It was available in just two colour combinations, with either Lagoon Green metallic or Mauritius Blue paintwork. The ten green cars all had a complete two-tone Nappa leather interior in Parchment and Light Parchment, and the ten blue cars all had a similar interior but in Silvergrey and Light Silvergrey. All had left-hand drive.

The bias of the Cecotto Edition was towards luxury equipment, and all cars came with an electric sunroof and rear sunblind, headlight washers and Servotronic steering. Inside, the front seats were heated and power-adjustable, with a memory on the driver's side, and the rear seats were also heated. The wood trim was in burr walnut, there were velour floor mats, and automatic climate control was standard. The original equipment radio was a BMW Bavaria C Business type.

Not surprisingly, a wide range of extra-cost options was on offer. Buyers could request 9 x 17-inch rear wheels, Shadowline body trim, a green-tinted windscreen strip and an M rear spoiler, and could, of course, ask for the M5 badge to be left off. Interior options were a driver's side airbag, a self-dimming rear view mirror, cruise control, rear reading lamps, power-adjustable rear headrests and (wisely) an alarm system. The radio could be upgraded to either the BMW Bavaria Electronic CD radio or the BMW Bavaria C Professional radio (with or without ten-disc CD changer), and a cassette storage box could be had as well.

The Winkelhock Edition

The Winkelhock Edition was very different, and was really a stripped-out lightweight model that also featured additional

---

THE NAGHI MOTORS SPECIAL EDITION

M5 enthusiasts are divided on the issue of whether the Naghi Motors special edition qualifies as a proper factory special edition or not. Either way, Naghi Motors, who were BMW's Saudi Arabian importers, asked for a special edition to be created from the last fifteen European-specification 3.6-litre M5s. The cars were built in late March and early April 1992; five in Alpine White II, five in Jet Black and five in Lagoon Green metallic.

The cars were built by BMW Motorsport with M System II 'throwing star' wheels from the 3.8-litre models, with the 9 x 17 size at the rear. All had Shadowline trim, a rear spoiler and a green windscreen sun strip. The front seats were Recaro sports types in Anthracite M cloth on black and white cars, or Neon Green and Anthracite striped cloth on green cars, in all cases with black leather bolsters and red safety belts. Air conditioning, velour floor mats, a Hirschmann phone antenna and a BMW Bavaria Cassette III ICE system were all fitted in Germany.

Naghi Motors then added touches of their own when the cars reached Saudi Arabia (and this is really why the cars' status as a legitimate special edition is disputed). These extra touches were door sill plates with the Naghi Motors name, a tri-colour M stripe on the leading edge of the bonnet on the driver's side, and a red leather steering wheel, gearshift grip and handbrake grip.

THE 3.6-LITRE E34 M5

performance equipment. There were fifty examples for sale to the public (plus one pre-production car to make fifty-one in total), all painted Jet Black with contrasting lower body panels in Sterling Silver metallic. The overall weight reduction was claimed to be 40kg (88 lb) as compared to a standard M5 at the time.

All these cars had Shadowline exterior trim, an electric sunroof and 9 x 17 rear wheels with wide tyres. Weight reduction was achieved by using a smaller battery (66 amps instead of 85 amps) and a smaller (80-litre) fuel tank, and by a number of deletions. The amount of sound-deadening material was reduced, and the electric rear windows, rear headrests, fog lights, headlight washers and vanity mirrors were all omitted.

Nevertheless, these cars were attractively trimmed. Velour floor mats and a BMW Bavaria C Business radio with hi-fi speaker system were standard. There were front sports seats in Anthracite M cloth with Black Nappa leather bolsters, red seat belts front and rear, and suede trim on the 385mm M-Technic II steering wheel, shift knob, gearshift boot and handbrake grip. The overall interior impression was similar to that on the 1990-model Sport Evolution version of the E30 M3. Few extras were offered, the list being limited to an M rear spoiler, a manually operated rear sunblind, the same ICE upgrades as the Cecotto edition and either air conditioning or automatic climate control; when either of these was ordered, a standard-size 85 amp battery was fitted.

PERFORMANCE FIGURES FOR THE E34 3.6-LITRE M5 MODELS

European saloon	0–60mph	6.3 sec
	Maximum	250km/h (155mph), electronically limited
US-spec saloon	0–60mph	6.4 sec
	Maximum	250km/h (155mph), electronically limited

Note that some road tests achieved even better times and speeds.

PRODUCTION TOTALS FOR THE E34 3.6-LITRE M5

A total of 8,383 3.6-litre cars were built, according to Thomas G. Müller in *Die Grosse BMW M Chronik*. This figure is at variance with figures published by BMW (see Note 2 below.)

Type	Build dates	Total
HD91	August 1988–January 1989	361
	January 1989–July 1991	5,000
	July 1991–April 1992	535
	(Sub-total)	**5,896**
HD92	December 1989–November 1991	531
	(Sub-total)	**531**
HD93	December 1989–March 1993	1,691
	(Sub-total)	**1,691**
HD98	June 1990–(unknown) 1992	265
	(Sub-total)	**265**
	Grand total	**8,383**

Notes:
(1) HD91 cars were European-specification LHD types
HD92 cars were European-specification RHD types (mainly for UK)
HD93 cars were North American-specification LHD types
HD98 cars were CKD types assembled in South Africa.
(2) BMW official figures show different build totals in three instances:
HD91   5,877
HD92   524
HD93   1,678
HD98   265 (unchanged)
to give a total of 8,344 cars.
(3) The South African cars left Germany in kit form between June 1990 and an unknown date in 1992, but were built up at Rosslyn between September 1990 and March 1993.
(4) Müller also notes that a further 36 cars were planned but not built.

PAINT AND UPHOLSTERY OPTIONS

September 1988 to August 1989

There were eight paint colours available in this period, of which five were metallics. Names are shown in their English forms.

Colour	Code	Colour	Code
Alpine White II	218	Malachite Green metallic	205
Black	086	Misano Red	236
Diamond Black metallic	181	Salmon Silver metallic	203
Macao Blue metallic	250	Sebring Gray metallic	229

In this period there were six interior options. Two featured cloth upholstery with Nappa leather bolsters (and became available from November 1988), one was a 'complete' leather style and the remaining three were 'extended' leather styles. Natur and Siam Grey were not available on the RHD HD92 models.

Colour	Code	Colour	Code
Anthracite M cloth	0313/0314/A8AT	Siam Gray extended Buffalo leather	0322
Natur complete Nappa leather	0321/L8NR	Silver Gray M cloth	0315/0416/A8SL
Natur extended Nappa leather	0320/L7NR	Silver Gray extended Nappa leather	0319

September 1989 to August 1990

There were again eight paint colours available in this period, of which five were metallics. Names are shown in their English forms.

Colour	Code	Colour	Code
Alpine White II	218	Jet Black	668
Brilliant Red	308	Macao Blue metallic	250
Calypso Red metallic	252	Sebring Gray metallic	229
Diamond Black metallic	181	Sterling Silver metallic	244

In this period there were nine interior options. Two featured cloth upholstery with Nappa leather bolsters, two were plain leather, two were 'complete' leather styles, and the remaining three were 'extended' leather styles. The two plain leather styles were for North America only (from December 1989) and the two 'complete' styles were not available on the RHD HD92 models. The 'extended' styles were available in Canada but not in the USA. On HD91 models from April 1990, the Nappa leather options could be had with Nappa Textil Webstruktur (option code 785) centre sections. On HD92 models, the option was available through the BMW Individual programme, but it was not available on North American models.

Colour	Code	Colour	Code
Anthracite M cloth	0313/0314/A8AT	Silver Gray M cloth	0315/0416/A8SL
Black Nappa leather	0226/0526	Silver Gray Nappa leather	0227
Black complete Nappa leather	0330/L8SW	Silver Gray complete Nappa leather	0331
Black extended Nappa leather	0318/L7SW	Silver Gray extended Nappa leather	0319
Champagne extended Nappa leather	0312/L7CM		

(continued overleaf)

■ THE 3.6-LITRE E34 M5

September 1990 to November 1991

Two more paint colours were added to the existing selection to make ten options in this period. Seven were metallics. Names are shown in their English forms.

Colour	Code	Colour	Code
Alpine White II	218	Lagoon Green metallic	266
Brilliant Red	308	Macao Blue metallic	250
Calypso Red metallic	252	Mauritius Blue metallic	287
Diamond Black metallic	181	Sebring Gray metallic	229
Jet Black	668	Sterling Silver metallic	244

There were ten interior options in this period. Two featured cloth with leather bolsters; two were plain leather; two were 'complete' leather; three were 'extended' leather; and there was just one with 'extended' Buffalo leather. All leather except the Buffalo type was Nappa. Neither the Buffalo leather nor the Black 'complete' leather could be had on RHD HD92 models. Standard for the USA was Light Silver Gray plain leather (which was not available anywhere else except Canada), and the three 'extended' options were available in Canada but not in the USA. Nappa Textil Webstruktur centre sections were available for leather upholstery as before.

Colour	Code	Colour	Code
Anthracite M cloth	0313/0314/A8AT	Champagne extended Nappa leather	0312/L7CM
Anthracite extended Buffalo leather	0418/M7AT	Light Silver Gray Nappa leather	0438/0527
Black Nappa leather	0226/0526	Light Silver Gray extended Nappa leather	0417/L7SH
Black complete Nappa leather	0330/L8SW	Light Silver Gray complete Nappa leather	0419/L8SH
Black extended Nappa leather	0318/L7SW	Silver Gray M cloth	0315/0416/A8SL

December 1991 to April 1992

There were thirteen paint colours for most of this period, of which ten were metallics. Avus Blue metallic was available only on North American cars. Names are shown in their English forms.

Colour	Code	Colour	Code
Alpine White II	218	Lagoon Green metallic	266
Avus Blue metallic	276	Macao Blue metallic	250
Brilliant Red	308	Mauritius Blue metallic	287
Calypso Red metallic	252	Sebring Gray metallic	229
Diamond Black metallic	181	Sterling Silver metallic	244
Jet Black	668		

There were ten interior options for most of this period. Two were plain leather; two were 'complete' leather; two were 'extended' leather; and there was just one with 'extended' Buffalo leather. All leather except the Buffalo type was Nappa. Neither the Buffalo leather nor the Black 'complete' leather could be had on RHD HD92 models. The three 'extended' options were available in Canada but not in the USA. Nappa Textil Webstruktur centre sections were available for leather upholstery as before.

Colour	Code	Colour	Code
Anthracite M cloth	0313/0314/A8AT	Champagne extended Nappa leather	0312/L7CM
Anthracite extended Buffalo leather	0418/M7AT	Light Silver Gray Nappa leather	0438/0527
Black Nappa leather	0226/0526	Light Silver Gray complete Nappa leather	0419/L8SH
Black complete Nappa leather	0330/L8SW	Light Silver Gray extended Nappa leather	0417/L7SH
Black extended Nappa leather	0318/L7SW	Silver Gray M cloth	0315/0416/A8SL

May 1992 to August 1993 (North American HD93 models only)

A limited selection of just five paint colours was available on the final North American 3.6-litre models. Three of these were metallics. Names are shown in their English forms.

Colour	Code	Colour	Code
Avus Blue metallic	276	Mugello Red	274
Calypso Red metallic	252	Sterling Silver metallic	244
Jet Black	668		

There were eight interior options in this period. All were leather. Two were plain leather; two were 'complete' leather; two were 'extended' leather; and there was just one with 'extended' Buffalo leather. All leather except the Buffalo type was Nappa. The three 'extended' options were available in Canada but not in the USA.

Colour	Code	Colour	Code
Anthracite extended Buffalo leather	0418/M7AT	Champagne extended Nappa leather	0312/L7CM
Black Nappa leather	0226/0526	Light Silver Gray Nappa leather	0438/0527
Black complete Nappa leather	0330/L8SW	Light Silver Gray complete Nappa leather	0419/L8SH
Black extended Nappa leather	0318/L7SW	Light Silver Gray extended Nappa leather	0417/L7SH

■ THE 3.6-LITRE E34 M5

E34 M5 3.6-LITRE SPECIFICATIONS

Engine:
Type S38 B36 6-cylinder petrol
3453cc (93.4mm x 86mm)
Twin overhead camshafts, chain-driven
Four valves per cylinder
Seven-bearing crankshaft
Compression ratio 10.0:1
Bosch Motronic electronic fuel injection
315PS (310bhp) at 6,900rpm   (311PS for North America)
360Nm (266lb ft) at 4,750rpm
Engines for most markets had a three-way ceramic exhaust catalyst and Lambda sensor, but those for the Gulf States had no exhaust catalyst and were consequently rated at 318PS.

Transmission:
Five-speed Getrag 280/5 manual gearbox
  Ratios 3.51:1, 2.08:1, 1.35:1, 1.00:1, 0.81:1

Axle ratio:
3.91:1 except:
3.73:1 on North American-specification cars from July 1991
(25 per cent limited-slip differential standard on all models)

Suspension, steering and brakes:
Front suspension with MacPherson struts, coil springs, gas dampers and 25mm anti-roll bar
Rear suspension with semi-trailing arms and auxiliary pivot link, coil spring struts, gas dampers, self-levelling and 18mm anti-roll bar
Speed-variable recirculating-ball steering with standard power assistance; ZF Servotronic speed-related steering available as an option
Disc brakes all round, 315mm (12.4in) ventilated on front wheels; 300mm (11.8in) solid on rear wheels to September 1989, thereafter 300mm ventilated rear discs; twin hydraulic circuits; ABS standard

Dimensions:
Overall length:	4,720mm (185.8in)
Overall width:	1,751mm (68.9in)
Overall height:	1,392mm (54.8in)
Wheelbase:	2,761mm (108.7in)

Wheels and tyres:
8J x 17 five-stud alloy wheels on 235/45ZR17 tyres
Optional 9J x 17 rear wheels with 255/40ZR17 tyres

Kerb weights:
European spec	1,720kg/3,792lb
US spec	1,744kg/3,845lb

CHAPTER FOUR

THE 3.8-LITRE E34 M5

The success of the M5 in the second half of the 1980s had made other car makers sit up and take notice, and by the start of the new decade BMW was facing the first volume-produced rivals for its high-performance saloon. At the Paris Motor Show in September 1990, arch-rival Mercedes-Benz announced its 500E model – based on the W124 medium saloon range that competed directly with BMW's 5 Series, and powered by a quad-cam 5-litre V8 engine that delivered 326PS. With its standard automatic gearbox, this car could hit 60mph in 5.9 seconds – a whole 0.4 seconds less than the 315PS 3.6-litre M5 with its manual gearbox.

Worse still was the new Opel Lotus Omega (sold as a Vauxhall Lotus Carlton in Britain). By enlarging its 6-cylinder engine to 3.6 litres and adding twin turbochargers, Opel had created a car with a massive 382PS that could hit 60mph from rest in 5.2 seconds and power on to a top speed of 176mph (283km/h). It may have been rather cruder than either the M5 or the Mercedes, but it was also considerably cheaper – and Opel had chosen not to subscribe to the gentlemen's agreement under which BMW and Mercedes limited their maximum speeds to 250km/h (155mph).

BMW had to do something to reclaim leadership of the high-performance super-saloon market, and what it did was

Serious opposition: the success of the M5 concept had prompted other makers to produce challengers. Above is the Mercedes-Benz 500E and, below, the Vauxhall Lotus Carlton. MERCEDES-BENZ UK (top) AND VAUXHALL MOTORS (bottom)

The 3.8-litre car was a mid-life upgrade for the E34 M5, and with it came an M5 Touring estate car that took the fight where other high-performance saloon makers had not yet gone. BMW

BELOW: A hoop spoiler was also made available for the 3.8-litre models, as seen here on a UK-market right-hand-drive car. In this case, the owner chose to have the M5 badge left off the boot lid.
NICK DIMBLEBY

ABOVE: Avus Blue metallic was one of the new paints available for the 3.8-litre models, although it was also offered on the final 3.6-litre types for North America. The contrast with the silver lower body panels is striking, and the 'throwing star' alloy wheels make this one of the best-looking M5 models ever. BMW

THE 3.8-LITRE E34 M5

to give the existing M5 a major boost by fitting a new and more powerful engine. The 3.8-litre E34 M5 was announced at the Frankfurt Motor Show in autumn 1991, although actual availability was not until spring of the following year. The car evened the score with Mercedes, taking the same 5.9 seconds to hit 60mph from rest. The Opel nevertheless had to remain the fastest road-going saloon for the moment, and even talk of the new M5's 170mph potential if derestricted could not match the Opel's verifiable maximum speed.

There was, though, an ace up BMW's sleeve. If the company could not match Mercedes by offering an automatic transmission, and could not match Opel for sheer performance, it could outflank both of them by offering an alternative body style. An M5 convertible had already been considered some years ago, and then rejected as a production choice. But in the meantime, BMW had been preparing an estate version of the E34 5 Series for introduction at the 1991 Frankfurt Motor Show. It was a relatively simple decision to create a Motorsport derivative of this to sell alongside the new 3.8-litre M5 saloon.

THE NEW 3.8-LITRE POWERTRAIN

Although nobody outside the company knew this yet, the new 3.8-litre engine would be the final development of the Motorsport division's original M88 24-valve 6-cylinder. The engine simply could not be enlarged any more and remain reliable. The Motorsport engineers increased the bore of the existing 3.6-litre S38 engine by 1.2mm and lengthened the stroke by 4mm to give a new swept volume of 3795cc. The new engine was known as an S38 B38 and could be distinguished from the 3.6-litre type by a grey cam cover surround where the older engine had a black one.

The increase in swept volume was just the start of this further development. The compression ratio was raised to 10.5:1, lighter pistons were used on shorter conrods, and room was found for larger inlet and exhaust valves. The latest version of the Bosch Motronic engine management system (version 3.3) had enough capacity to permit two further important changes: first, the traditional distributor was

The 3.8-litre engine would be the final version of the S38 24-valve 'six'. Although it looked much like the 3.6-litre engine, there were some clear differences. Compare this picture with the 3.6-litre engine shown on page 49 and note, for example, the different style of rocker box cover with its relocated oil filler cap. NICK DIMBLEBY

■ THE 3.8-LITRE E34 M5

eliminated in favour of a separate coil for each cylinder, each fired by the engine management system; and second, the electronic manifold resonance flap system could be refined to give even better torque response. One result was that the new engine not only had 11 per cent more torque than the old at its peak, but also delivered more than 71 per cent of that torque as low down the rev range as 1,800rpm.

This made for greater flexibility, smoother progress in traffic and, of course, gave more of the effortless acceleration so beloved of M5 drivers.

Subsidiary changes played their part, too. The exhaust manifold of the S38 B38 engine was specially developed using a high-grade superalloy called Inconel, which up to that point had been used mainly in extreme environments such as Formula 1 and NASCAR exhaust systems, and in the Space Shuttle programme. The throttle bodies were also enlarged. The crankshaft damper on the front of the engine was redesigned, and a new dual-mass flywheel was added, the two between them giving even smoother operation of the new engine.

In standard form, with new all-metal catalytic converters designed by the Motorsport division and giving lower back pressure, the 3.8-litre engine delivered 340PS at 6,900rpm and 400Nm of torque at 4,750rpm, both figures slightly further round the rev counter than the maxima of the 3.6-litre engine it replaced. However, different demands in different countries meant that there had to be some special versions of the engine as well. Emissions regulations in Austria and Switzerland demanded a different 338PS tune, and there was a low-compression version of the engine for the Gulf States. Very noticeable was that the 3.8-litre engine was never homologated for the USA. With hindsight, it looks as if that points to something of a rush to get it into production after news of the Mercedes and Opel super-saloons reached Munich.

Once again, the five-speed Getrag manual gearbox was pressed into service as the only option, being carried over unchanged from the 3.6-litre car. The same 3.91:1 final drive was retained, and once again a 25 per cent limited-slip differential was a standard feature.

THE REVISED CHASSIS

The revised M5 also benefited from further chassis development, and it might be reason-

Only on the 3.8-litre engine was there an M logo on the air inlet box. AUTHOR

THE 3.8-LITRE E34 M5

able to suppose that this had been done as part of the normal development process within the Motorsport division rather than specifically for the 3.8-litre car. The new model was fitted as standard with a system called Adaptive M-Technic suspension, which was really the Motorsport division's own development of the EDC III system available on other BMW models. The name indicated that it was the third generation of the company's Electronic Damper Control system.

Adaptive M-Technic suspension used sensors to monitor the road speed, steering input, acceleration or deceleration, and lateral body movements, and was then able to adjust the rates of the dampers within a fraction of a second to the most suitable of three different settings. The result was a constant variation of damping to give both a comfortable ride and taut handling, without the compromises inherent in systems dependent on a single damper rate.

The standard steering remained as before, with power assistance that varied according to engine speed. The ZF Servotronic system that varied assistance according to road speed remained an extra-cost option, but it was also available as part of the Nürburgring Package, so called after the legendary race-track in the Eifel mountains where BMW did much of its vehicle testing.

The Nürburgring Package added wider 9 x 17-inch wheels at the rear, with fatter 255/40ZR17 tyres, a thicker 19mm rear anti-roll bar, and a dashboard control switch for the Adaptive M-Technic suspension that allowed the dampers to be locked at their hardest setting for optimum handling. Available on both saloon and Touring models of the M5, it differed slightly between the two models. The Touring estates already had the 9 x 17 rear wheels as standard, and when the package was ordered their rear anti-roll bar was increased to 20mm in diameter.

EXTERIOR FEATURES

The basic appearance of the E34 M5 saloon of course remained the same as it had been for the 3.6-litre models, but the Motorsport division introduced a pair of straightforward changes that made the two cars look very different indeed. One was that the lower body panels changed in colour: although Diamond Black metallic remained available, Granite Silver metallic replaced the earlier Sebring Grey metallic. This new lighter colour gave a strikingly different appearance to those cars that had it.

The second change was to the wheels, although it was actually less of a change than it appeared on the surface. The 3.8-litre cars came with a further development of the M System multi-part wheels known as M System II. The load-bearing wheel was again a black-painted five-spoke alloy, but this time the outer cover also had five spokes, a design that actually blew cooling air onto the brake discs even more efficiently than the first version. That outer cover also had a very striking design, which BMW enthusiasts everywhere have taken to calling the 'throwing star' pattern, and it made a big difference to the appearance of the 3.8-litre cars.

The 'throwing star' or M System II wheels had a striking design, but behind the removable covers had the same five-spoke alloy wheel as the earlier M System I type. NICK DIMBLEBY

The optional aero mirrors with their two narrow mounting arms were an attractive feature that was made standard on some models. NICK DIMBLEBY

■ THE 3.8-LITRE E34 M5

A single exhaust pipe would never do for an M5, so the 3.8-litre cars had twin pipes, neatly mounted so that they did not hang below the bodywork. MAGIC CAR PICS

These wheels were also fitted on some special versions of the late 3.6-litre cars, as Chapter 3 explains. Unlike the M System I wheels, they were also used outside the M5 range, notably on a late North American model called the 540i Sport that went some way towards filling the gap left by the absence of an M5 in North America after 1993.

The exterior changes also included a new range of paint colours, and among these were two colours that would remain unique to the Motorsport division: Avus Blue and Daytona Violet, which reflected two of the three colours in the famous M tricolour logo. Options now included aerodynamic door mirrors, although it appears that these were not available in all countries where the M5 was sold.

INTERIOR FEATURES

The transformation would not have been complete without some changes inside the passenger cabin as well. The first things noticeable on opening a door were the new sill plates with a more prominent M5 logo. However, the main difference from the interior of the 3.6-litre cars lay in the style of the standard cloth upholstery, which now had a different 'rain-striped' fabric in grey or black allied to bolsters and head restraints covered in Amaretta synthetic suede instead of leather.

As before, there were three styles of leather available, each one more costly than the last and each one using Nappa leather. Once again, they were known simply as leather, extended leather and complete leather, and there was a Buffalo leather option as well.

A new feature on the E34 cars was the automatic climate control system, advanced and costly enough to be an option even on the M5. Its drum-type rotary controls are seen here on the dashboard of a German-market car. NICK DIMBLEBY

THE 3.8-LITRE E34 M5

ABOVE: **Imaginative use of light and dark shades of grey made the dashboard of the 3.8-litre M5 particularly attractive. This is a right-hand-drive UK car with cloth seats.** MAGIC CAR PICS

RIGHT: **This was the 'rain-stripe' style of upholstery that came with the leather option, seen here on the rear seats.** BMW

■ THE 3.8-LITRE E34 M5

The E34 M5 Touring looked just like its practical mainstream equivalent – unless you noticed those wheels, the jutting front air dam, and the M5 badge on the grille. BMW

THE M5 TOURING

The signs are that the decision to introduce the Touring as a second M5 derivative was made rather late in the day. The car may even have still been under development when it was shown at Frankfurt in October 1991, as production examples took another six months to begin reaching customers.

That motor show was also where the Touring body derivative made its debut for the rest of the BMW range. It became the first-ever factory-built 5 Series estate car from BMW, and was made available with a variety of different engines. BMW's aim was to tap into the strong market for large estate cars that was already being exploited by Mercedes-Benz, Volvo and the French makers Peugeot and Citroën – none of whom, of course, offered a high-performance derivative. The name Touring was chosen partly because of its distinctiveness and partly as an echo of the well-liked BMW 2002 Touring hatchback model that had been available between 1971 and 1974.

The Touring body was superbly styled, its rear section and third side window being exceptionally well integrated into the established shape of the E34 range. It was still often the case in the early 1990s that estate cars were designed as modifications of an existing saloon, and that became apparent in their less-than-happy lines. However, BMW had followed the Mercedes-Benz example of designing an estate derivative alongside the saloon. The result was that there were fewer compromises in the finished product.

At speed, few of the Touring model's distinctive M5 characteristics were readily visible, and that was the way the customers liked it. BMW

THE 3.8-LITRE E34 M5

TOP: **The centre of the dashboard was still angled towards the driver and that steering wheel had an attractive three-spoke design.** MAGIC CAR PICS

MIDDLE: **Was this the perfect Q-car? The dark paint means that the dark lower panels are barely noticeable, and this German-market M5 Touring has been de-badged. Only the wheels hint that this might be an M5. The door mirrors with their more aerodynamic design were an extra-cost option, even on the M5.** NICK DIMBLEBY

BOTTOM: **The twin sunroofs of the M5 Touring came from the options list of the mainstream estate models. The design was ingenious, but if the two panels got out of sync with one another, problems could arise.** BMW

The Touring models not only had a longer roof than the saloons, but also a different and slightly raised roof line. The window frames of the rear side doors were different from the saloon items to suit this and to blend in with the third window on each side. A sloping tailgate hinged in the conventional fashion from the roof, but a BMW innovation was that the glass section could be opened separately from the main panel, allowing smaller items to be stowed more easily and quickly. Other refinements were electrically assisted catches for this window and for the tailgate itself, and a washer jet that appeared from the panelwork when needed.

Inside, the load floor had four retractable luggage securing points, and underneath it was concealed a useful additional storage compartment.

73

■ THE 3.8-LITRE E34 M5

The rear seat of course folded forwards to increase the load space available in the rear, but it was asymmetrically split so that long loads could be carried on one side while passengers occupied either one or two of the rear seat positions. Two rear head restraints were standard, and a third in the centre was optional. The contents of the luggage area could be concealed under a neat roller blind, and options included a load space liner and, inevitably, a dog guard.

In most respects, the M5 Touring was really a 5 Series Touring with the mechanical and cosmetic elements of the M5 saloon added to it. So all examples had the 3.8-litre S38 B38 engine, the five-speed Getrag gearbox, the M5's additional front spoilers and its special paintwork with contrasting lower panels. One special feature was that all the Touring models had 9 x 17-inch rear wheels with 255/40ZR17 tyres as standard, with a 19mm anti-roll bar, so that the optional Nürburgring Package brought only a thicker anti-roll bar (of 20mm diameter) and the locking button for the M Adaptive dampers. An ingenious double sunroof, shared with the mainstream Touring models where it was an option, was also available.

It may have been a reflection of the haste with which the M5 Touring was created that no right-hand-drive models were ever made available. (A small number have nevertheless been created by specialists out of left-hand-drive cars.) In fact, the M5 Touring was never very numerous, and only 891 cars were built in three and a half years of production, or rather less than 23 per cent of all 3.8-litre E34 types. The M5 Touring has the distinction of being the last new model from the Motorsport division to be built by hand; all subsequent models have been designed to be assembled in greater volumes on BMW's main assembly lines.

PRODUCTION CHANGES

There were just a small number of production changes in the first few years of 3.8-litre M5 production, but a series of major changes arrived in May 1994. Before then, side impact bars and an anti-theft engine immobilizer had been standardized in September 1992 (and some countries, such as Britain, had gained the aerodynamic door mirrors as standard

The last of the 3.8-litre cars, built after May 1994, had a new design of double-spoke wheels with an 18-inch diameter. This Arctic Silver metallic car has the lower panels in contrasting black. BMW

THE 3.8-LITRE E34 M5

equipment). From September 1993, a driver's airbag became standard for all countries, which meant that the three-spoke steering wheel gave way to a four-spoke type with tricolour Motorsport stitching on its rim.

The May 1994 changes included both a facelift and mechanical changes, and affected both saloon and Touring models of the M5. The revised models were easily recognizable by two key features – a wider grille that no longer carried an M5 badge, and a new style of road wheels. These wheels were single-piece alloys with five paired or split spokes and an 18-inch diameter, and were known as the M Parallel Spoke type. All models now had the staggered wheel-size arrangement formerly associated only with the Nürburgring Package and the Touring derivatives. They had 8-inch rims at the front and 9-inch rims at the rear; the tyres were nevertheless 245/40ZR18s on all four wheels.

The extra inch of diameter in these wheels reflected the trend towards larger and larger wheels that allowed designers to make maximum use of the wheel itself as an element in the overall design. More important for the Motorsport division, though, was that larger wheels also permit larger brakes, and the May 1994 revisions brought 345mm (13.6in) front and 325mm (12.8in) rear discs, ventilated in each case. The front discs also had a new two-piece design with a different material for their centre sections that allowed better heat dissipation from the 'floating' discs; this was a world-first application of the type to a road car.

The major mechanical change, however, was to a six-speed gearbox. Six-speed types were uncommon in 1994, although in this case BMW was playing catch-up because the Opel Lotus Omega had used one made by ZF. BMW stayed

The final models of the E34 M5 had these M Parallel Spoke wheels with an 18-inch diameter. MAGIC CAR PICS

This late 3.8-litre car shows the hooped spoiler and M Parallel Spoke wheels, plus what would now be seen as a period accessory: an aerial mounted through the rear window glass for a mobile phone installation. MAGIC CAR PICS

■ THE 3.8-LITRE E34 M5

with Getrag as a supplier, taking their type D gearbox and matching it to a taller final drive of 3.23:1.

The Nürburgring Package disappeared as an option, because most of its elements were now standard; only the Servotronic steering remained an extra-cost option after May 1994. The staggered wheel arrangement has already been mentioned, and now the saloons took on the 19mm rear anti-roll bar that had been part of that package, while the Touring models came as standard with the 20mm anti-roll bar. Even the lock-out control for the electronic dampers of the Adaptive M suspension was now fitted as standard.

This was the final evolution of the E34 M5, although there would be some special run-out editions just before production ended in July 1995, and these are described later. After the last cars had been built, there would be a gap of three years before BMW announced a new M5 model, but demand for a high-performance BMW four-door saloon was so great that the company was obliged to bridge that gap by creating a four-door saloon edition of the smaller M3.

THE RHD CARS

The left-hand-drive or HC91 models of the M5 vastly outnumbered the right-hand-drive or HC92 types, just as left-hand-drive 3.6-litre cars had been the more numerous. As for the HJ91 Touring models, these were built only with left-hand drive. The exact production figures are still in dispute, but either 343 or 373 cars were built with right-hand drive out of a saloon total of 3,019 (or 3,127); this gives a figure of

A CHANGE OF NAME

BMW Motorsport GmbH changed its name to BMW M GmbH in 1993, a year or so before the last of the 3.8-litre E34 M5s were built.

There were several business reasons for the change, but one was undoubtedly the strength of the M brand. Another was that BMW had longer-term plans to give the M division a wider remit. In future, it would be responsible not only for motorsport activities but also for much of the bespoke work on production vehicles – including, of course, the M5 itself.

WHAT THE PRESS THOUGHT

Autocar, 22 July 1992

'The wheel rethink makes the M5 look meaner, sharper and less frilly … the M5 you see now looks more like what you get: the world's swiftest and most capable saloon car.'

'While lacking the agility and rapier response of an M3, the M5 snaps into bends with superb economy of motion. Its steering isn't the last word in clearly resolved feel and the chassis' grip, while outstanding, isn't overwhelming.'

'The tyres are occasionally tempted to follow cambers and white lines.'

'The suspension always feels firm but supple and well damped, especially at high speed … [but] the tyres … are far from quiet, drumming and thrumming over coarse surfaces.'

'Overall, the new M5 is appreciably more refined than its predecessor.'

somewhere between 8.3 per cent and 11.3 per cent of the total for right-hand-drive 3.8-litre saloons.

Despite this low percentage of right-hand-drive models, there is no doubting BMW's commitment to building them. In fact, it appears that production of right-hand-drive saloons started in November 1991, some four months before full production of left-hand-drive cars! Nor was Britain the only country to take these models, as only sixty were built for the British market in the first year of production, or rather less than 60 per cent of that year's right-hand-drive build total. Production of right-hand-drive models stopped a month before that of other 3.8-litre types, in June 1995.

SPECIAL EDITIONS OF THE 3.8-LITRE E34 M5

The two special editions of the 3.6-litre M5 in 1991 made clear that such marketing tactics worked for the M5 just as well as they had done for the M3. So three further special

THE 3.8-LITRE E34 M5

editions were based on the 3.8-litre models, two of them on the saloon and one of them on the Touring.

The 20 Jahre Motorsport Edition

The 20 Jahre Motorsport Edition was a European special edition that went on sale in October 1992. There were twenty cars, all left-hand-drive saloons and all with an individually numbered plaque mounted on the centre console. Ostensibly, they celebrated twenty years of the Motorsport division, which had been established in 1972.

All twenty cars were intended to be Mugello Red with Jet Black lower panels, Shadowline trim and M System II wheels with Jet Black 'spokes'. In fact, the first car, which appeared at motor shows, was painted a different shade of bright red! An electric sunroof was standard, as were headlamp washers and M-Technic aerodynamic door mirrors. The passenger cabin had a number of special features, beginning with a driver's side airbag, automatic air conditioning, and a BMW Bavaria Cassette III ICE system. There were red seatbelts with BMW Motorsport lettering, Recaro sports front seats, and special M cloth upholstery with bolsters in Anthracite Amaretta. Alcantara suede with red stitching was used for the steering wheel rim, the gearshift grip and shroud, and for the handbrake grip.

The UK Limited Edition

In the UK, traditionally a strong market for the M5, the end of E34 M5 production was commemorated with a limited edition of fifty cars that is generally described simply as the UK Limited Edition. The plan was originally to call them the Steve Soper Edition, after the BMW racing driver, but the plan was abandoned at the last minute.

These saloons were built between March and June 1995, and were the last right-hand-drive models built. There were thirty-five cars with Orinoco metallic paint, and fifteen in Rosso Red. The Orinoco cars had a two-tone Petrol and Mint extended Nappa leather interior with bird's-eye maple wood trim in Graphite, and the red cars had extended Champagne leather with Natural Poplar wood trim. All had an electric sunroof, Shadowline exterior trim, headlight

Mugello Red was one of the two colour options for the UK Limited Edition. DAVE SMITH

77

■ THE 3.8-LITRE E34 M5

The UK Limited Edition was attractively finished with light wood and light-coloured upholstery. Note the limited-edition plate on the centre console, ahead of the gear lever. This was car number twenty of the fifty made. DAVE SMITH

washers and a green-tinted windscreen band, a three-spoke airbag steering wheel, electrically adjustable front seats and air conditioning. Five cars were additionally supplied with Servotronic steering. Other special features were a storage net in the passenger's footwell, unique wooden gearshift and handbrake grips, and a numbered limited-edition plate on the centre console.

The Elekta Edition

The only special edition of the Touring model was created at the request of a group of dealers in Italy, and was known as the Elekta Edition. The cars were built in 1995 and were the last twenty M5 Touring models destined for Italy; they were created with the help of the BMW Individual custom-building scheme.

Ten of the cars were painted British Racing Green, and ten were in Sterling Silver metallic; both had Shadowline exterior trim, headlamp washers and the otherwise optional roof rails and twin electric sunroofs. The green cars had Hazelnut extended leather upholstery and Mexico Green carpets, and the silver ones had Marine Blue extended leather with matching carpets. The dashboard and upper door panels were in black leather, and there was a storage net in the passenger's footwell.

Inside the passenger cabin, the special features were a three-spoke airbag steering wheel, electrically adjustable front seats with a memory on the driver's side, a self-dimming rear view mirror and automatic climate control. A high-quality ICE speaker system was installed, but the head unit was left to the customer's choice. The gearshift grip also had a metal insert bearing the Elekta name and the car's number within the limited edition.

Some M5 enthusiasts prefer not to recognise the Elekta Edition as a proper BMW limited edition, mainly because its specification was not created within BMW.

THE 3.8-LITRE E34 M5

ABOVE: **The Elekta Edition was specially prepared for a group of Italian dealers, and was the only special edition based on the Touring model.** DOMINIC FRASER

The interior of the Elekta Edition was largely standard, but there was a special insert for the gearshift grip. Note that the total was shown in Roman numerals (**XX** for 20) while the individual number (in this case, 06) was shown in **Arabic** figures. DOMINIC FRASER

79

A 3.8-litre M5 became the 'Ring Taxi' that took visitors around the famous Nürburgring race track during 1992. At this stage, the M5 was still a product of the Motorsport division, and the car was stickered up accordingly. Just visible in this picture is the internal rollover cage. BMW

Deprived of a 3.8-litre M5, which was never homologated for North America, US customers made do with a 540i Sport model, featuring the latest 4.0-litre V8 engine and the M5's 'throwing star' alloy wheels. BMW

PRODUCTION TOTALS FOR THE E34 3.8-LITRE M5

A total of 3,910 cars was built according to BMW official figures, but see Note 2 below.

Type	Build dates	Total
HC91	March 1992–July 1995	2,676
HC92	November 1991–June 1995	343
	(Saloon sub-total)	**3,019**
HJ91	March 1992–July 1995	891
	(Touring sub-total)	**891**
	Grand total	**3,910**

Notes:
(1) HC91 cars were European-specification LHD saloons
HC92 cars were European-specification RHD saloons
HJ91 cars were European-specification LHD Touring models.
(2) The build totals shown are those provided by BMW. The serial number batches suggest greater numbers were built – or, at least, planned.
There is no clear explanation for this discrepancy. If every serial number in the batches had been used on a car, the build totals would have been as follows:
HC91   2,754
HC92   373   (Saloon sub-total 3,127)
HJ91   944   (Grand total 4,071)
(3) The BMW M Registry has also obtained figures for the six-speed models built from May 1994:
HC91   404
HC92   139   (Saloon sub-total 543)
HJ91   209   (Grand total 752)

PERFORMANCE FIGURES FOR E34 3.8-LITRE M5 MODELS

Saloon	0–60mph	5.7 sec
	Maximum	250km/h (155mph), electronically limited
Touring	0–60mph	5.9 sec
	Maximum	250km/h (155mph), electronically limited

E34 M5 3.8-LITRE SPECIFICATIONS

Engine:
Type S38 B38 6-cylinder petrol
3795cc (94.6mm x 90mm)
Twin overhead camshafts, chain-driven (duplex chain)
Four valves per cylinder
Seven-bearing crankshaft
Compression ratio 10.5:1; there was a low-compression engine for the Gulf States
Bosch Motronic M3.3 engine management system
Exhaust with catalytic converter and Lambda sensor
340PS (335bhp) at 6,900rpm
400Nm (295lb ft) at 4,750rpm
Austrian and Swiss models initially had 338PS (334bhp) and later 331PS (327bhp); no figures are available for the low-compression Gulf States engine

Transmission:
Five-speed Getrag 280/5 manual gearbox to April 1994
    Ratios 3.51:1, 2.08:1, 1.35:1, 1.00:1, 0.81:1
Six-speed Getrag type D manual gearbox from May 1994
Ratios 4.23:1, 2.52:1, 1.66:1, 1.22:1, 1.00:1, 0.83:1

Axle ratio:
3.91:1 with five-speed gearbox
3.23:1 with six-speed gearbox
(25 per cent limited-slip differential standard on all models)

Suspension, steering and brakes:
Front suspension with MacPherson struts, coil springs, gas dampers and anti-roll bar
Rear suspension with semi-trailing arms, auxiliary pivot link, coil spring struts, gas dampers and anti-roll bar; 18mm anti-roll bar on saloon and 19mm anti-roll bar on Touring up to April 1994; 19mm anti-roll bar on saloon and 20mm on Touring with Nürburgring Package to April 1994 and standardized from May 1994
Speed-variable recirculating-ball steering with standard power assistance; ZF Servotronic speed-related steering available as an option
Disc brakes all round, 315mm (12.4in) ventilated on front wheels and 300mm (11.8in) ventilated on rear wheels, to April 1994; 345mm (13.6in) ventilated 'floating' front discs and 325mm (12.8in) ventilated rear discs from May 1994. Twin hydraulic circuits; ABS standard

Dimensions:
Overall length:	4,720mm (185.8in)	Overall width:	1,751mm (68.9in)
Overall height:	1,392mm (54.8in)	Wheelbase:	2,761mm (108.7in)

Wheels and tyres:
To April 1994:
8J x 17 five-stud alloy wheels with 235/45 ZR 17 tyres
9J x 17 five-stud alloy wheels with 255/40 ZR 17 tyres standard on rear wheels of Touring models and optional (with Nürburgring Package) on rear wheels of saloons
From May 1994:
8J x 18 (front) and 9J x 18 (rear) five-stud alloy wheels with 245/40 ZR18 tyres on all models

Kerb weights:
Saloon	1,720kg (3,792lb)
Touring	1,800kg (3,968lb)

■ THE 3.8-LITRE E34 M5

PAINT OPTIONS

December 1991 to August 1992
There were twelve paint colours in this period, of which seven were metallics. Names are shown in their English forms.

Colour	Code	Colour	Code
Alpine White II	218	Diamond Black metallic	181
Avus Blue metallic	276	Granite Silver metallic	237
Brilliant Red	308	Jet Black	668
Calypso Red metallic	252	Lagoon Green metallic	266

September 1992 to August 1993
There were ten paint colours in this period, of which seven were metallics. Names are shown in their English forms.

Colour	Code	Colour	Code
Alpine White II	218	Granite Silver metallic	237
Avus Blue metallic	276	Jet Black	668
Calypso Red metallic	252	Lagoon Green metallic	266
Daytona Violet metallic	283	Mugello Red	274
Diamond Black metallic	181	Sterling Silver metallic	244

September 1993 to April 1994
There were again ten paint colours in this period, of which seven were metallics; note the change to Alpine White III from Alpine White II. Names are shown in their English forms.

Colour	Code	Colour	Code
Alpine White III	300	Fjord Grey metallic	310
Avus Blue metallic	276	Jet Black	668
Calypso Red metallic	252	Mugello Red	274
Daytona Violet metallic	283	Oxford Green metallic	324
Diamond Black metallic	181	Sterling Silver metallic	244

May 1994 to August 1995
There were ten paint colours in this period, of which seven were metallics. Avus Blue was discontinued early, in July 1995. Names are shown in their English forms.

Colour	Code	Colour	Code
Alpine White III	300	Cosmos Black metallic	303
Arctic Silver metallic	309	Daytona Violet metallic	283
Avus Blue metallic	276	Fjord Grey metallic	310
Bright Red	314	Jet Black	668
Calypso Red metallic	252	Oxford Green metallic	324

THE 3.8-LITRE E34 M5

UPHOLSTERY OPTIONS

December 1991 to February 1992

There were eight interior options for most of this period. Two featured cloth with Amaretta synthetic suede bolsters; two were 'complete' leather; three were 'extended' leather; and there was just one with 'extended' Buffalo leather. All leather except the Buffalo type was Nappa. Neither the Buffalo leather nor the Black 'complete' leather could be had on RHD HC92 models. Note that codes 0330, 0418 and 0419 were available only on HC91 models, and that 0312 and 0417 appear not to have been available on HJ91 (Touring) models.

Colour	Code	Colour	Code
Anthracite M cloth	0475/A9AT	Champagne extended Nappa leather	0312/L7CM
Anthracite extended Buffalo leather	0418/M7AT	Light Silver Gray complete Nappa leather	0419/L8SH
Black complete Nappa leather	0330/L8SW	Light Silver Gray extended Nappa leather	0417/L7SH
Black extended Nappa leather	0318/L7SW	Silver Gray M cloth	0476/A9SL

March 1992 to August 1995

The eight existing options were joined by three more to give a total of eleven choices. One (Champagne complete Nappa leather) was available on all models, but the two new two-tone options were available on Touring models only.

Colour	Code	Colour	Code
Anthracite M cloth	0475/A9AT	Light Parchment with Dark Parchment extended Nappa leather	0494/N3PE
Anthracite extended Buffalo leather	0418/M7AT	Light Silver Gray complete Nappa leather	0419/L8SH
Black complete Nappa leather	0330/L8SW	Light Silver Gray extended Nappa leather	0417/L7SH
Black extended Nappa leather	0318/L7SW	Light Silver Gray with Dark Silver Gray extended Nappa leather	0493/N3SH
Champagne complete Nappa leather	0321/L8CM	Silver Gray M cloth	0476/A9SL
Champagne extended Nappa leather	0312/L7CM		

CHAPTER FIVE

E39 M5 – THE FIRST V8

The buying public had to wait what felt like an inordinately long time before a replacement for the E34 M5 reached the showrooms. The last of those cars had been built in mid-1995; the new E39 5 Series range was announced in October that year, giving buyers at least an idea of what the eventual new M5 might look like; but it would not be until the Geneva Motor Show in March 1998 that the E39-based M5 was previewed. Even then, it was simply that – a preview. The cars did not actually go on sale until October that year, very nearly three years after the last of the E34 M5s had been built.

Well before the new models became available, there had been rumours that the new car would have a V8 engine instead of the long-established Motorsport 'six'. It was in any case a simple deduction to make, because it was clear that the S38 6-cylinder could not be enlarged any further to find more power, and because BMW had announced V8 engines for the largest-capacity variants of the final E34 models. Some observers felt that a V8 was in any case necessary to counter the V8-engined Mercedes-Benz E500 (née 500E) and whatever might follow it.

These cars were on sale for a period of five years, from autumn 1998 to summer 2003. In that time, BMW built 20,482 examples – vastly more than had been made of any earlier M5. The M5 was now big business, and yet it still remained a rare and desirable piece of property. The success of the E39 version proved as much of a tribute to BMW's marketing skills as to the development skills of the company's Motorsport division.

THE E39 5 SERIES

With the E34 5 Series, BMW had drawn almost level with Mercedes in the public estimation, if not yet in sales. So with the next-generation 5 Series, the company made a very determined attempt to close the gap. It required an enormous investment, which BMW later claimed was 1,000

The mainstream E39 saloons had a much more curvaceous outline than earlier 5 Series models, and one that to some eyes took acclimatization.
AUTOCAR, PRESS PICTURE VIA NEWSPRESS

E39 M5 – THE FIRST V8

million Deutschmarks, or £446 million at 1995 exchange rates.

By this stage, the 5 Series had become quite literally central to the whole BMW product programme. As the mid-range saloon, it was positioned between the smaller 3 Series and the larger 7 Series, and it was the main weapon in BMW's attempt to wrest leadership of the German domestic market from Mercedes-Benz. So the new car had to be not just good, but excellent. The brief given to Munich's engineers in the early 1990s was to make the new 5 Series ride better, handle better, go faster, use less fuel and be safer in an accident than the E34. It was a formidable challenge.

The BMW and Mercedes new-model replacement programmes overlapped to some degree, and it was Mercedes who renewed their mid-range saloons first, with the W210 E-Class range announced in June 1995. Almost immediately afterwards, BMW issued some 'taster' pictures of its forthcoming new saloon, and in October 1995 it was formally introduced at the Frankfurt Motor Show.

The E39s were quickly acknowledged as the best in their class – superior, even, to the E-Class Mercedes – and as raising standards in the medium-saloon sector. Over the next few months, they went on to claim award after award from the motor industry and motoring press.

The E39's curvaceous new shape had been developed under BMW's styling chief Chris Bangle. Several design cues reflected the established E36 3 Series cars and the latest E38 7 Series models, such as the sleek nose with headlamps and turn indicators behind flush-fitting glass lenses. From this more rounded nose, the lines of the bonnet swept back in a broad and purposeful 'power bulge' to join steeply raked windscreen pillars. Past the traditional BMW dog's-leg shape of the rear side window, the rear window pillar led down to a boot that was higher than the bonnet, for the E39 had a wedge-shaped profile.

The new car was bigger than its predecessor – longer by 55mm (2in), wider by 49mm (1.9in) and taller by 23mm (0.9in). An extra 69mm (2.7in) in the wheelbase brought an extra inch of rear legroom, and overall the car was 20 per cent more aerodynamic than the E34s had been. Its bodyshell was also a massive 82 per cent stiffer, thanks to the high-strength steel and aluminium used in its construction.

Changes for the M5 were subtle, but very effective in giving the E39 shape a slightly harder edge. In this picture, the front apron, wheels, door mirrors and Shadowline window frames are all obviously different. A closer look shows the M5 badge on the front door bump-strip, and the clear lenses for front and side indicator lights. BMW

■ E39 M5 – THE FIRST V8

A rear view of the same car shows that there were clear indicator lenses at the rear, too. The E39 was the model that introduced the four exhaust tailpipes that have since become an M5 signature. This car does not have the rear spoiler, and it is not immediately obvious from the picture that the rear wheels have wider rims than those on the front. BMW

In crash tests, the E39 exceeded all legislative safety requirements then current, and yet, incredibly, the bodyshell was no heavier than the E34 type.

Further weight was saved by using aluminium alloy for several elements of the suspension – a world first on a volume production car. The sub-frames, too, were of lightweight aluminium alloy. Careful positioning of components and detail engineering solutions resulted in a front-to-rear weight distribution that was close to the 50/50 ideal, which made an important contribution to both ride comfort and handling. For the first time on a 5 Series BMW, there was a rack-and-pinion steering system to give more positive steering feel (although, as explained later, this was not carried over for the M5 model), and the rear suspension incorporated a version of the semi-active 'elasto-kinematic' rear suspension that had been developed within the Motorsport division for the E34 M5 models. The rear suspension also incorporated pneumatic self-levelling struts and the ASC + T (Automatic Stability Control and Traction) system came as standard, though with a disabling switch to suit driver preferences. EDC III variable damper control was also an option.

When it was fitted, the tail spoiler was as discreet as ever. A first glance at this car would probably not reveal it at all. BMW

The neat and stylish dashboard moulding incorporated the usual clear set of dials under a binnacle, and both passenger's and driver's airbags were standard equipment. There was a thermostatically controlled heating and ventilating system with a pollen filter as standard, and an innovative latent-heat reservoir in the front passenger's footwell stored waste heat from the engine to speed up heater response and to help the engine warm up faster after a cold start. The ICE system, concealed under a dashboard flap for security, used a non-standard size unique to the E39 in order to deter thieves.

A further important element in the design of the E39 models was the use of the latest 'bus' electronics systems, as pioneered on the E38 7 Series cars. The increasing use of electrical systems to pass information from one control module to the next around the car had begun to present problems in the complexity and size of the wiring harness, and the E39 followed BMW's new solution of using a bus network to simplify these systems; essentially, a simple communications wire linking the different modules carried all the necessary signals around the circuit.

Beyond that, an incredible array of options and features enabled each customer to tailor a car to taste. These included AIC rain-sensing wipers (which adjusted their speed automatically to suit the level of rainfall), a fold-out zipped bag that would take two pairs of adult skis, and a multi-function steering wheel that contained a number of auxiliary controls – at that stage a very new device just pioneered on the 7 Series cars. Even in standard form, the E39s were comprehensively equipped.

CREATING THE E39 M5

When work began on the M5 version of the E39 5 Series, the E34 model then in production was available as both a saloon and a Touring estate. The E39 5 Series was also planned with a Touring derivative, and the Motorsport division certainly worked on creating M5 derivatives of both the saloon and the estate. However, E34 M5 Touring sales were never very strong (they amounted to just under 23 per cent of world-

A Touring version of the M5 was worked up into prototype form, and at least one car was built. However, BMW decided against putting it into production. BMW

■ E39 M5 – THE FIRST V8

wide sales annually) and BMW top management decided against bringing a Touring version of the E39 M5 to market. The decision was attributed to unspecified financial considerations – probably fears that sales would not justify the additional expense and trouble.

That a Touring version of the M5 was considered is undeniable, however. At least one prototype was built, and in February 2010 it was revealed to the public as part of the celebrations associated with the twenty-fifth anniversary of the M5. The car, painted in Titanium Silver and featuring a Black leather interior, still exists as part of the BMW historic collection.

So only the saloon model was taken forward to production. Right from the start of the E39 M5 project, BMW appears to have been looking for ways in which it could increase production of its successful high-performance saloon, and its choice fell on transferring its assembly from the BMW M plant in Garching to the main assembly lines in Dingolfing. Taking such a car from being a hand-finished model to a small-volume, line-built derivative of a volume-built car meant that the car had to be designed for what was in effect mass production. Although the consequences of this were almost entirely undetectable in the finished product, it was noticeable in the simplified range of paint and trim options for the E39 M5, and also in the total absence of any factory-built special editions over the five years of production.

Of course, the heart of the third-generation M5 would be a new engine, and the specially developed V8 is discussed in more detail later. But it was important to make the E39 saloon look distinctive, too. Beginning at the front of the car, the Motorsport team added an enlarged grille with thicker bright-metal frames, but followed the example of the last E34 M5s and did not add an M5 logo to it. Next came a different front spoiler (branded M-Technic, naturally) with a large central air intake protected by wire mesh. Clear turn

More testing: the slippery shape of the E39 was refined even further for the M5 by wind-tunnel testing. The smoke trail shows the passage of air over the top of the car. MAGIC CAR PICS

E39 M5 – THE FIRST V8

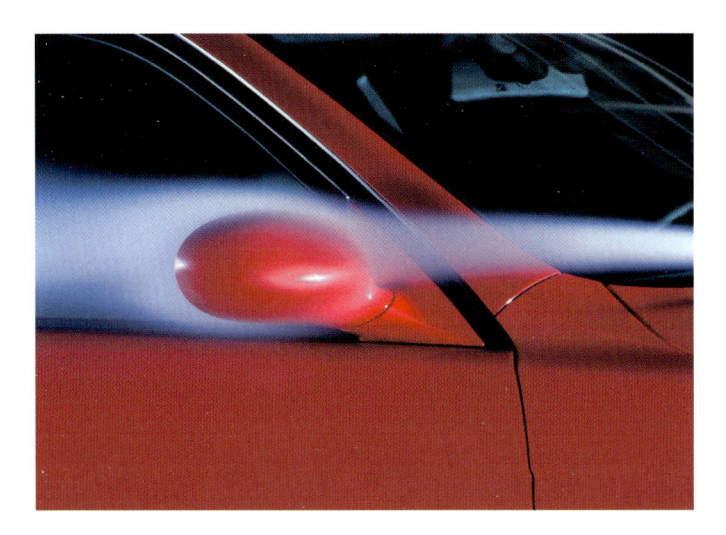

Even the design of the M5's door mirrors was optimised in the wind tunnel. MAGIC CAR PICS

The door mirrors could also be folded up electrically to help protect them from damage when the car was parked. MAGIC CAR PICS

indicator lenses were specified both front and rear, where ordinary E39s had amber lenses.

An electric glass sunroof was an option unique to the M5, although other E39s could have a metal sunroof as an option. Special door mirrors were complemented by a power-folding mechanism designed to keep them out of harm's way when the car was parked. Like all E39s, the M5 had rubber side bump-strips, but in this case the mouldings carried an M5 logo on each front door. Shadowline window trim was made standard, although in practice the bright metal trim used on ordinary E39s could be had to order at no extra cost. The car had a special rear bumper with a lower diffuser that neatly framed the two pairs of exhaust outlet pipes; the rear bumper could be fitted at extra cost with a Park Distance Control system. The boot lid meanwhile came with a small lip spoiler painted in the body colour. Both this and the discreet M5 logo on the trailing edge of the lid could be deleted on request.

Special alloy wheels were also drawn up as part of the package. These had ten sets of paired spokes and an 18-inch diameter, and were known as M Parallel Spoke II types. They had a Satin Chrome finish and, following the lead set by the final E34 M5 models, they had wider rims and tyres at the rear to sharpen handling.

All the cars came with Xenon headlights and a headlight wash system, both of these drawn from the options list for the mainstream E39s. A satellite navigation system was made available at extra cost, and an electrically operated rear sunblind could also be ordered. Generally, the E39 M5s came with a very high standard of optional equipment – the way most buyers seemed to like them.

THE E39 M5'S POWERTRAIN

The figures associated with the new V8 engine could hardly have been more memorable. BMW claimed 400PS (394bhp) at 6,600rpm and 500Nm (369lb ft) at 3,800rpm, and the swept volume of 4941cc enabled it to call it a 5-litre engine. It was surely no coincidence that the engine in the rival Mercedes E500 (which ceased production in 1995) had been a 5-litre V8, with a slightly larger 4973cc capacity but just 326PS and 480Nm. With this new engine, BMW had comprehensively beaten those figures and raised the stakes in the high-performance saloon sector of the market.

Like the M88 engine that sired the S38 range of 6-cylinders, the new Motorsport V8 engine had been developed from a production engine. The starting-point for its design was BMW's all-aluminium M62 engine, itself developed from the 4-valve M60 V8s first introduced in 1992. There were M62 engines in the E39 535i, with a 3498cc swept volume, and 540i, with a 4398cc swept volume.

The similarities between the volume-production M62 engine and the M derivative, which took the S62 name, allowed the new M5 engine to be assembled at the main Dingolfing assembly plant instead of at the M division's Garching

■ E39 M5 – THE FIRST V8

ABOVE: **The new V8 engine was hidden under another of BMW's cosmetic cover panels, but the M logo at the front and the twin air filter boxes gave the whole thing a purposeful look.** BMW

BMW was clearly aware that the M Power legend only read properly from the side of the car, and issued this press picture, perhaps as a way of making amends. BMW

90

E39 M5 – THE FIRST V8

plant. However, there were far more differences between them than this manufacturing rationalization might suggest. In fact, BMW claimed that the S62 engine of the E39 M5 was more than 95 per cent new.

A larger swept volume of 4941cc came from a 2mm bore increase with a 6.3mm stroke increase, and that figure was rounded up to 5 litres in the new engine's full code of S62 B50. The compression ratio was raised to 11:1 from the 10:1 of the M62, and this high compression was matched by special head gaskets made of three layers of steel. The risk of misfires was entrusted to a new 32-bit digital engine management system developed in conjunction with Siemens and called the MSS 52.

The MSS 52 system of course took care of traditional engine management functions such as precise control of the fuel injection and the ignition timing. It also allowed BMW to create a true 'drive-by-wire' system, because it interpreted signals from a sensor on the accelerator and translated them into instructions that were delivered to each of the eight throttle bodies; there was no accelerator cable in the traditional sense. Better yet, the MSS 52 introduced new possibilities, and BMW made full use of them. One was the incorporation of two alternative throttle response modes, enabling the driver to press a Sport button on the dashboard that switched to a rapid-response mode for maximum acceleration. BMW called this M Driving Dynamics.

The greater capabilities of MSS 52 also enabled BMW to use what it called Double-VANOS for the first time on any engine. VANOS stands for VAriable NOckenwellen Steuerung, or Variable Camshaft Control, and

This view of the S63 B50 engine gives a better idea of the way it really looked. The two cylinder banks, arranged in a 90-degree vee, can be clearly seen. BMW

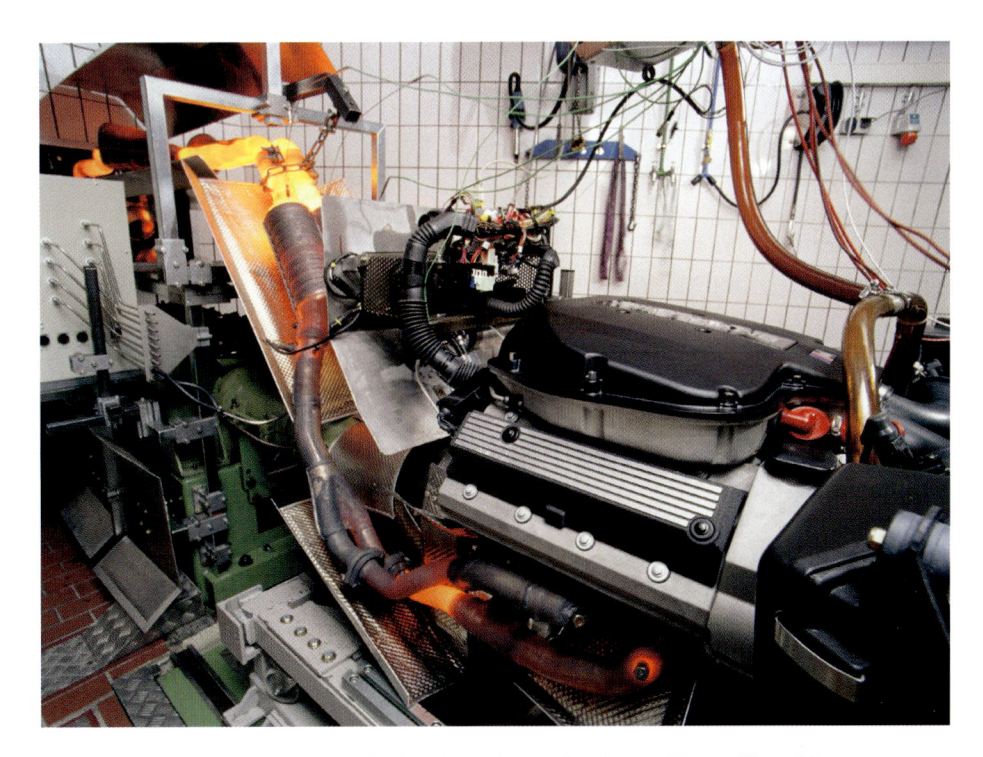

The V8 engine is seen during bench testing here. Tests like this were obviously followed by endurance testing in the prototype cars. MAGIC CAR PICS

■ E39 M5 – THE FIRST V8

Once again keen to demonstrate the special features of the new M5 as well as it could through the media, BMW issued this picture showing the V8 engine with its catalytic converters and dual exhaust system terminating in those four tailpipes, each with its own silencer. BMW

was already available on production engines where it typically enabled the inlet timing to be continuously varied to suit demand on the engine. However, things were a little more complex on the V8, which already had four overhead camshafts in its M62 form. For the S62, VANOS was added to all four camshafts, and to guard against likely problems, the M62's single-row timing chain was replaced by a double-row chain.

The camshafts themselves had a special hollow design to assist lubrication, and the Motorsport engine also boasted a pioneering oil system that was sensitive to G-forces and had not one but two scavenger pumps, one acting on each cylinder bank. There was also a heat exchanger between the oil and coolant systems to guard against excessive temperatures if the engine was used hard, and this was backed up by a high-capacity water pump.

Both the inlet and exhaust systems differed from those on the parent M62 engine. There was a dual air induction system, complemented by a complex exhaust manifold arrangement with individual butterfly valves on each cylinder bank to smooth out gas flow. A free-flow exhaust system incorporated twin catalytic converters and was arranged to emerge under the rear apron in four exhaust outlets. Finally, the M division had made sure that this engine would not only work well and sound good, but would also look good under the bonnet. So it was given a large central top cover with the M logo and the legend M Power against a fake carbon-fibre background.

As they had on the final E34 M5s, BMW entrusted transmission of all this power and torque to a Getrag six-speed manual gearbox. The same gearbox was in fact already available behind the M62 engine in the 540i models of the E39, but the rest of the drivetrain was altered to suit the M5. The changes consisted of a stronger clutch and a taller 3.15:1 final drive, the latter incorporating a 25 per cent limited-slip differential as was now traditional for M5 models.

THE E39 M5'S STEERING, SUSPENSION AND BRAKES

There was just one disappointment in the specification of the new M5, and that lay in the steering. Although the mainstream E39 models mostly had a sharp and responsive rack-and-pinion system, the M5 was brought to market with a recirculating-ball type. This was necessary because the V8 engine did not leave enough room for a power-assisted rack, and the V8-engined 535i and 540i models had to suffer the same steering system. However, the Motorsport engineers had done their best, and the M5 boasted a quicker steering ratio (14.7:1 instead of 17.9:1) and came with ZF Servotronic speed-related variable power assistance as standard.

E39 M5 – THE FIRST V8

Most of the differences between the M5 and the mainstream E39s were under the skin, and BMW issued this 'ghost' image when the cars were launched to show where the differences lay. For a clearer look at the essential mechanical elements, as the second picture shows, they 'removed' the body. BMW

93

■ E39 M5 – THE FIRST V8

The weight of the steering could even be varied to suit the driver's taste, and the so-called Sport button on the centre console provided higher levels of resistance to steering inputs for fast driving.

Like the mainstream E39s, the M5 had high levels of aluminium in its suspension, reducing unsprung weight to improve both ride and handling. However, the car rode lower on springs that were 23mm (0.9in) shorter than the standard E39 type, and it also had different damper settings. Both front and rear anti-roll bars were fatter than standard, and there were polythene auxiliary springs instead of the standard rubber type. At the front, the steering gear, body mountings and thrust bearings were all reinforced, and there were special wheel bearings as well. The rear suspension, meanwhile, had steel ball-joints instead of the standard rubber bushes. Finally, the BMW parts store had been raided to find stronger components that were already available, and the M5 shared its lower rear control arms with the Touring versions of the E39 and its rear integral link with the 750iL version of the E38 model.

To rein in the excesses of less skilled drivers not used to the M5's power, the E39 models also came with DSC (Dynamic Stability Control). This was a traction control system that incorporated the earlier ASC (Automatic Stability Control) system but through the ABS system could also brake any wheel individually to help correct either oversteer or understeer. This was the first time such a system had been used on any car from the M division, and BMW was well aware that it was likely to be accused of 'nannying' its customers. So it provided a button on the centre console that switched the system off, leaving the driver to exercise his skill (or discover his lack of it) in the traditional way.

Servo-assisted all-disc brakes with a dual circuit ABS system were part of the basic E39 architecture, and the M5 simply built on that. The Motorsport engineers added larger brake discs all round, ventilated front and rear, and carried over the composite construction of the front discs that had been used successfully on the later E34 M5 models.

THE E39 M5'S INTERIOR

The basic architecture of the E39's interior could not, of course, be changed for the M5 models, but there was a great deal in its detail appointments that could be altered to provide the unique features that M5 enthusiasts – like those for the other M models – so loved. Special door sill plates

The instrument panel carries just the one M logo, on the 300km/h speedometer, and there are red needles and aluminium bezels to help make the M5 more special inside. The stitching on the steering wheel rim is in the tricolours of the M division. BMW

The increasing complexity of the car's on-board systems led to a profusion of buttons and switches, which could be quite confusing for the driver. This M5 does not have the monitor screen that was an optional extra. BMW

with the M5 logo and an M-branded driver's footrest were just the beginning.

The instrument panel incorporated a whole host of special features. Most immediately obvious were that the dials had red needles and aluminium bezels, and that the speedometer with its M logo was calibrated to 300km/h or 180mph (even though the car was speed-limited as standard to 250km/h or 155mph). The rev counter, meanwhile, was a very special confection with an oil temperature gauge where other E39s had an econometer and an ingenious moving LED redline that discouraged the driver from using high revs until the engine had reached full working temperature – when the LEDs were extinguished automatically.

The steering wheel of course incorporated an airbag, and was a three-spoke design with a 375mm diameter and M tricolour stitching on the rim; like that on other E39s, it was a multi-function type, in this case with buttons on the upper spokes for the ICE system and the cruise control. As in the E34 M5s, the top of the gearshift grip incorporated the M logo and was illuminated, but for the E39 the grip itself could be had in three styles. These were leather with aluminium-look, Bruyere Club wood or Burr Walnut wood trim, in each case to match the trim style chosen for the rest of the interior.

To simplify manufacture, the M5 also came with a range of standard equipment that was drawn from the options

This was the Exclusive interior option, with leather upholstery and wood trim. In this guise, the M5 appealed to those who expected it to be a luxury car first and foremost. Just visible is the optional car telephone on top of the centre console box. BMW

■ E39 M5 – THE FIRST V8

ABOVE: **A quite different interior ambience was created by the Sport option. The seats have larger bolsters and a very different style from those associated with the Exclusive interior.** MAGIC CAR PICS

LEFT: **The all-black facia of this later US-model E39 is strikingly different from the gentle greys of the E34 3.8-litre car pictured on page 71. Note how all the switch graphics light up, and how the buttons on the multi-function steering wheel are differently arranged from those in the picture of an early car. The additional graphic on the far right of the dashboard is not original to the car.** TERABASS/WIKIMEDIA

list for other E39s. So the front seats were power-operated as standard and boasted a three-position memory on the driver's side. Like the mainstream E39s, the M5 could be ordered at extra cost with split-folding rear seats and a hatch for long loads in the rear bulkhead. The steering column could be tilted and telescoped electrically, and both cruise control and automatic climate control were standard. The on-board computer fitted as standard to all E39s was specified with its optional extended range of functions, and of course there was a top-quality ICE system.

Most interesting was that the new car was made available with alternative cabin styles. BMW had been aware for some time that M5 customers fell into two camps – those who saw it as a luxury car and those who valued its sporting qualities more highly – and had used the 1991 Cecotto and Winkelhock special editions of the E34 M5 to explore how both sides might best be satisfied. For the E39 M5, the outcome was the options of Sport and Exclusive trims.

Buyers could order the Sport interior with three basic combinations. One featured Alcantara upholstery and door panels with Nappa leather bolsters and aluminium-look trim. The other two both had Nappa Point leather upholstery and door panels with Nappa leather bolsters, the difference being whether aluminium-look or Bruyere Club wood trim was specified. The Exclusive interior trim meanwhile came with pleated Nappa leather and door trim, plus either Bruyere Club wood trim or Burr Walnut wood trim.

All five of these basic options could be had in three different styles. Standard was the basic style; above that and at extra cost came Extended Leather and Complete Leather. Extended leather brought leather on the centre console, door and centre armrests, door pulls and sun visors, and Complete Leather added to this leather on the door panels and upper door trims, the dashboard top, glovebox lid and lower B-pillars. With the Complete Leather interior, Alcantara was used for the headlining, windscreen pillars, upper B-pillars, C-pillars and the rear parcels shelf.

PRODUCTION CHANGES FOR THE E39 M5

There were no major mechanical changes to the M5 in its five-year production run, which of course minimized manufacturing problems and maximized profits for BMW. However, there were a few minor changes, and the start of the 2001 model-year in September 2000 brought the nearest thing the E39 models ever had to a makeover.

Early on in production, the cars took on an oval-shaped self-dimming rear view mirror. There were then changes to

Grey instrument faces were a feature of the 2001 facelift for the E39 M5. UNITY MEDIA

the paint options in September 1999 (coinciding with the M5's launch in North America), in March 2000, and again in September 2001. September 2001 was when the mainstream E39 cars had a facelift, taking on some of the features that had been pioneered on the M5 a year earlier. The final M5 change came in September 2002 for the 2003 model-year, when a DVD-based navigation system was standardized.

The 2001-model M5s were readily recognizable from the light units. Not only were the rear light units different, featuring a fast-response system made by Hella and known as Celis, but the headlights now came with light-conducting 'corona' rings that functioned as sidelights. This was an early instance of lights being used as an element in styling, and it proved very popular indeed, even attracting its own nickname of 'Angel Eyes'. The rear Park Distance Control was matched by a set of sensors embedded in the front bumper at the same time.

Although the passenger cabin remained unchanged in its essentials, there were several detail changes. Immediately obvious were a new three-spoke steering wheel with a thicker rim and different spoke design, in fact borrowed from the E46 M3 models. Grey instrument faces and a larger 165mm (6.5-inch) monitor screen that came with a new navigation and ICE system also attracted attention. Altogether less visible were an improved solar sensor for the automatic climate control system, and rear head-protection airbags concealed behind the headlining. A wireless Bluetooth car telephone connection system replaced the earlier cable-connected system. In the boot, meanwhile, the M Mobility tyre repair system was now supplied in an improved second-generation version.

Other changes affected the options. The Complete Leather interiors had always come with an Alcantara headlining, and now the less expensive Extended Leather interiors did, too. Then, for extra cost, buyers could order a new M Audio System with special tweeters, carbon-Kevlar coaxial speakers and two sub-woofers located behind the rear of the centre console.

THE RHD CARS

Production of right-hand-drive cars began at the same time as that of left-hand-drive models for Europe. They were known as DE92 models, to distinguish them from the DE91 (left-hand-drive European) and DE93 (North American specification) types.

WHAT THE PRESS THOUGHT

Road & Track, February 1999

'An automobile of utterly high performance, yet one that's equally at home just toodling around as well.'

'I found the M5 displaying uncanny stability – and relative tranquillity – on the Autobahn, even with its speedo touching 260km/h, a slightly optimistic interpretation of the M5's electronically limited 155mph maximum.'

Autocar, 20 January 1999

'In real terms, it's as quick as a 1756kg four-seater has ever been, Lotus Carlton included.'

'The gear-change feels … imprecise when rushed.'

'[The handling of] this car is exactly what an M car should be: no compromise. A car that is aimed squarely at the enthusiast, not at the middle ground audience.'

'Such is the M5's power and torque that it can kick its tail out on a damp road in any of the first three gears.'

'Without question the M5's chassis is the M division's greatest triumph in recent memory. Indeed, it's hard to find any serious fault in it.'

'Quite simply, the new car is the most impressive high-performance luxury saloon we've ever driven … It achieves this accolade because of the thoroughness of its development and the fact that in not one area could it be significantly improved.'

Wheels, May 1999

'The BMW M5 is its V8 engine. You feel it, you hear it and you cravingly use every kilowatt from it. The heart, the soul … your pleasure. All warm and fuzzy.'

'The M5 V8 sounds eternally angry, grumpy and is neither.'

'Through sweeping bends, you get the feel for the M5's weight and ways on the road. The steering, still recirculating ball not the more accurate rack and pinion, speaks to you.'

E39 M5 – THE FIRST V8

There were 2,595 E39 M5s with right-hand drive, and the majority of these were delivered in the UK. According to a very useful posting on www.m5portal.com, the UK took 1,952 cars. There were then 235 for Australia and 297 for South Africa, leaving 111 spread around various other markets where right-hand drive was required. Although Japan is a right-hand-drive country, all M5s delivered there had left-hand drive because of the extra prestige associated with such vehicles among Japanese enthusiasts.

THE NORTH AMERICAN CARS

North American sales, and primarily those in the USA, were an essential focus when the E39 M5 was being designed. That BMW got the recipe about right is abundantly clear from the overall sales figures for the model: there were 9,918 examples sold in North America, a figure that represents very nearly half of all the 20,482 cars built. The figure also translates as approximately 2,480 North American sales in every one of the four years when the car was available, a figure worth comparing with North American sales of the earlier E34 M5, which had totalled just 1,691 cars in four years for an annual average of about 422 cars.

To settle further quibbles among enthusiasts, it appears that there were 9,224 cars for the USA and 694 for Canada. However, the total figure of 9,918 falls short of the 9,992 cars actually built to the DE93 or North American specification, and the remaining seventy-four cars were delivered in

Differences between the European and North American cars were kept to a minimum. This North American model can be recognized by the outer edges of its front light units. The turn signal has a separate round amber lens, and the amber corner section houses the side marker light required by US Federal law. BMW

E39 M5 – THE FIRST V8

various other countries where European-specification cars were inappropriate for one reason or another.

The manufacturing rationalization that BMW had applied when designing the E39 M5 had begun earlier, as the E39 range itself was being drawn up. The key was to minimize differences between the European and North American cars, to reduce complication on the assembly lines and to reduce manufacturing costs as well. So the North American cars, coded internally as DE93 cars, were barely different from their European counterparts. They were introduced in September 1999 as 2000 models, around a year after they had first appeared in Europe.

The main visual differences were very small – simply running-lights in the bumper wraparounds of North American models. All the DE93 cars nevertheless came with the electric glass sunroof that was an extra-cost option in Europe. Less visibly, the exhaust catalysts were positioned closer to the engine to reduce warm-up times, and the North American models did not have the composite front brake discs that were standard on the European cars.

On the inside, the optional satellite navigation system was made standard on North American cars, and the Alcantara upholstery option was not made available, with the result that all DE93 cars had leather upholstery of one sort or another. What Europe knew as the 'Exclusive' interior trim was also rebranded as 'Luxury' in North America. All the cars also came with an M Driving Experience course at one of the BMW Performance Centers included in the showroom price.

A few specification changes were introduced over the years. So the revised navigation and ICE unit with its 165mm (6.5-inch) monitor screen became standard in autumn 2000 on the 2001 DE93 cars. Then the formerly optional 'auto headlamps' system became standard for the 2002 models, and finally the rear side airbags and split-folding rear seat were standardized on the 2003 models from September 2002. Production of North American-specification DE93 cars continued until the end, the last examples being built in June 2003 alongside the last European E39 M5s.

PRODUCTION TOTALS FOR THE E39 M5

There were 20,482 E39 cars in all.

Type	Build dates	Total
DE91	October 1998–June 2003	7,895
DE92	October 1998–June 2003	2,595
DE93	September 1999–June 2003	9,992

Grand total 20,482

Notes:
DE91 cars were European-specification LHD saloons
DE92 cars were European-specification RHD saloons
DE93 cars were North American-specification saloons

PERFORMANCE FIGURES FOR E39 M5 MODELS

All models	0–60mph	4.8 sec
	Maximum	250km/h (155mph), electronically limited

Without its speed limiter (which could be removed to special order outside Germany), the E39 M5 is supposedly capable of 300km/h (186mph).

E39 M5 SPECIFICATIONS

Engine:
Type S62 B50 V8-cylinder petrol
4941cc (94mm x 89mm)
Four overhead camshafts, chain-driven (duplex chain)
Four valves per cylinder
Five-bearing crankshaft
Compression ratio 11.0:1
Siemens MSS 52 engine management system
Exhaust with dual catalytic converters
400PS (394bhp) at 6,600rpm
500Nm (369lb ft) at 3,800rpm

Transmission:
Six-speed Getrag type D manual gearbox
   Ratios 4.23:1, 2.52:1, 1.66:1, 1.22:1, 1.00:1, 0.83:1

Axle ratio:
3.15:1
(25 per cent limited-slip differential standard on all models)

Suspension, steering and brakes:
Front suspension with double-joint MacPherson struts, aluminium control arms, gas dampers and anti-roll bar
Multi-link rear suspension with coil springs, gas dampers and anti-roll bar
Speed-variable ZF Servotronic recirculating-ball steering with 14.7:1 ratio and standard power assistance
Disc brakes all round, 345mm (13.58in) ventilated on front wheels and 328mm (12.91in) ventilated on rear wheels; 'floating' two-piece front discs on European-specification cars; twin hydraulic circuits; ABS standard

Dimensions:
Overall length:	4,783mm (188.3in)
Overall width:	1,801mm (70.9in)
Overall height:	1,412mm (55.6in)
Wheelbase:	2,830mm (111.4in)

Wheels and tyres:
8J x 18 five-stud alloy front wheels with 245/40ZR18 tyres
9.5J x 18 five-stud alloy rear wheels with 275/35ZR18 tyres

Kerb weights:
Saloon   1,826kg (4,026lb)

■ E39 M5 – THE FIRST V8

PAINT AND UPHOLSTERY OPTIONS

Names are shown in their English forms throughout.

October 1998 to August 1999

There were nine paint colours available in this period.

Colour	Code	Colour	Code
Alpine White III	300	Jet Black	668
Anthracite metallic	397	Oxford Green metallic	324
Avus Blue metallic	276	Royal Red metallic	390
Carbon Black metallic	416	Silverstone metallic	425
Imola Red II	405		

Note: Oxford Green metallic appears not to have been available on North American models.

September 1999 to February 2000

There were ten paint colours available in this period. Eight were the same as in the previous period. Oxford Green metallic was replaced by Oxford Green metallic II (code 430), and Titanium Silver metallic (code 354) was added to the list. This second version of Oxford Green metallic was available on North American cars.

March 2000 to August 2001

There were again ten paint colours available in this period. Nine were the same as in the previous period; Le Mans Blue metallic replaced Avus Blue metallic.

Colour	Code	Colour	Code
Alpine White III	300	Le Mans Blue metallic	381
Anthracite metallic	397	Oxford Green metallic II	430
Carbon Black metallic	416	Royal Red metallic	390
Imola Red II	405	Silverstone metallic	425
Jet Black	668	Titanium Silver metallic	354

September 2001 to June 2003

There were again ten paint colours available in this period. Seven were the same as in the previous period; Blue Water metallic replaced Silverstone metallic, Chiaretto Red metallic replaced Royal Red metallic, and Sterling Grey metallic replaced Anthracite metallic.

Colour	Code	Colour	Code
Alpine White III	300	Jet Black	668
Blue Water metallic	896	Le Mans Blue metallic	381
Carbon Black metallic	416	Oxford Green metallic II	430
Chiaretto Red metallic	894	Sterling Grey metallic	472
Imola Red II	405	Titanium Silver metallic	354

There were fifteen interior trim options for the E39 M5, and no new ones were introduced. One option (Anthracite M-Texture Alcantara with Black extended Nappa leather) was available on Canadian DE93 models, but not on those for the USA. The full range was as follows:

Colour	Code	Colour	Code
Anthracite M-Texture Alcantara with Black extended Nappa leather	F2AT	English Green extended Nappa Heritage leather	M3EG
Black complete Nappa Heritage leather	MISW	Imola Red with Black complete Nappa Point leather	O6IM
Black extended Nappa Heritage leather	M3SW	Imola Red with Black extended Nappa Point leather	O5IM
Black complete Nappa Point leather	O6SW	Le Mans Blue with Black complete Nappa Point leather	O6LB
Black extended Nappa Point leather	O5SW	Le Mans Blue with Black extended Nappa Point leather	O5LB
Caramel complete Nappa Heritage leather	MICR	Silverstone with Black complete Nappa Point leather	O6SS
Caramel extended Nappa Heritage leather	M3CR	Silverstone with Black extended Nappa Point leather	O5SS
English Green complete Nappa Heritage leather	MIEG		

From August 2000, a reduced range of options was available on DE93 models. There were nine for Canada and eight for the USA.

Colour	Code	Colour	Code
Anthracite M-Texture Alcantara with Black extended Nappa leather	F2AT	Imola Red with Black extended Nappa Point leather	O5IM
Black complete Nappa Heritage leather	MISW	Le Mans Blue with Black complete Nappa Point leather	O6LB
Black extended Nappa Point leather	O5SW	Le Mans Blue with Black extended Nappa Point leather	O5LB
Caramel complete Nappa Heritage leather	MICR	Silverstone with Black extended Nappa Point leather	O5SS
Imola Red with Black complete Nappa Point leather	O6IM		

CHAPTER SIX

THE E60 AND E61 V10 MODELS

Once again, BMW made its M5 customers wait for a replacement model. The E39 cars went out of production in June 2003, and by that time the world had already been introduced to the mainstream models of the new E60 5 Series, which was revealed at the Geneva Show in March 2003. There would be no sign of a new M5 for another year, however, until BMW presented a 'teaser' M5 Concept at Geneva in March 2004. This was pretty much the real thing, which was then announced in September that year at the Paris Motor Show, but few buyers got their hands on one before the start of 2005. It had been a long wait.

The market had also changed more than a little since the days of the E39's conception. BMW's decision not to produce a Touring variant of that model had left the field wide open to their competitors, and both Audi and Mercedes-Benz had entered the fray with high-performance deriva-

A lower ride height and flared sill panels gave the M5 derivative of the E60 a more aggressive stance, in which those big wheels also played an important part. Door mirrors were quite different, although their bodies again had blacked-out lower sections, and the M5 had a completely different front air dam that incorporated larger, sculpted air intakes. Note also the 'gills' or side vents on the widened front wings. BMW

THE E60 AND E61 V10 MODELS

The rear view had all the design cues expected of an M5 – the special rear apron with four tailpipes, a large central diffuser and, of course, that badge. The 'fin' on the roof housed aerials for the ICE, telephone and satellite navigation systems. BMW

tives of their mid-size estate cars. Audi had the RS6 Avant from 2002, and Mercedes fielded its supercharged E55 AMG estate from 2003. BMW did respond, but was not able to get an M5 Touring into the public domain until the Geneva Show in March 2007. This was based on the E61 companion model to the E60 saloon versions of the 5 Series.

When the new E60-based M5 was announced in 2004, it immediately claimed the title of the world's fastest production four-door saloon. Maximum speed was of course limited to 250km/h (155mph) under the German manufacturers' agreement, but with a 4.8-second 0–60mph time the car was simply blisteringly fast. It also broke new ground in several areas. Engines with a V10 configuration were rare indeed, the pioneer in this area having been the Dodge Viper of 1991, and the E60 M5 now followed suit with BMW's first road-car V10 engine. The car was also the first to have a seven-speed version of the Sequential Manual Gearbox, initially introduced in 1996 in six-speed form for the E36 M3 models.

This fourth-generation M5 built upon the success of its predecessors to become the most numerous M5 so far – but only just. There had been 20,482 E39 M5s, and there were 20,582 of the E60 and E61 cars. That figure divided into 19,564 E60 saloons (so, fewer than the E39s, which were all saloons) and 1,025 (just under 5 per cent) Touring estates. Figures from BMW show that the US market took the lion's share of production with 8,800 cars, all of them saloons. The second strongest market was Great Britain and Ireland combined, which took 1,776 cars, more than the 1,647 sold in BMW's own German domestic market.

THE E60 5 SERIES

For the next generation of its 5 Series mid-range saloon, BMW developed a car that was larger in all dimensions than the E39, the key aim being to achieve more cabin and boot space. The development programme began in 1997 and the car entered production with the usual wide range of engine options in March 2003. It came initially with a choice between six-speed manual and Steptronic automatic gearboxes, and the huge variety of options offered a great deal of advanced electronic technology that included a simplified version of the controversial iDrive system used in the E65 7 Series cars.

The E60 shape was quite rounded, although very different from that of the earlier E39, and was always somewhat controversial. Design was led by Davide Arcangeli working

■ THE E60 AND E61 V10 MODELS

The mainstream E60 saloon was characterized by flat sections on top of the headlight units and by a 'bustle-back' boot shape, the latter characteristic of designer Chris Bangle. BMW

To get the handling balance right for the E60, BMW used aluminium extensively in the front end of the bodyshell. The M5 did the same. It was an ingenious solution, but it did make for expensive repairs after a front-end shunt. BMW

THE E60 AND E61 V10 MODELS

to design chief Chris Bangle. The body was constructed with extensive use of aluminium in front of the engine bulkhead while the centre and rear sections were of steel, in order to achieve a 50:50 front-to-rear weight distribution. Early cars achieved only a three-star rating in the Euro NCAP crash safety tests, so BMW made some detail changes and the car obtained a four-star score on its retest. That aluminium front end proved to be something of a liability in service, as it increased the cost of major front end repairs considerably.

The E60 platform was designed for multiple uses, and in due course was also used for the E63 and E64 6 Series coupés, as a well as a special long-wheelbase 5 Series built for the Chinese market. A closer derivative was the E61 Touring model that was introduced alongside the saloon. An innovative feature was the use of run-flat tyres as standard on all mainstream models.

The E60 range was given its mid-life makeover in 2007, which in BMW-speak was called its LCI (Life Cycle Impulse). This brought a new front bumper, fog lights, headlights, tail lights and boot, together with a minor facelift to the interior and a series of new engines. Also central to this set of changes were a number of fuel-saving technologies under the heading of Efficient Dynamics.

EXTERIOR DESIGN OF THE E60 AND E61 M5

Like the E39s they replaced, the E60 and E61 models of the M5 were built on the main BMW assembly lines at Dingolfing, and not in the workshops of the BMW M Division.

The E60 M5 models were assembled at Dingolfing, in the same assembly hall as the other E60 5 Series cars. This is the powertrain and suspension laid out on an assembly trolley early in the assembly process. BMW

■ THE E60 AND E61 V10 MODELS

The Touring or E61 model of the M5 looks smaller than it really was in this static picture of a UK-market right-hand-drive model. In the rear view, its real size is more apparent. This was a practical estate car, as well as an M5. KHEDARA ARIYARATNE/WIKIMEDIA AND BMW

THE E60 AND E61 V10 MODELS

The carefully sculpted shapes of the air intakes in the front apron are clear in this picture; normally, the area between grille and air intake is occupied by a registration plate. BMW

The jewel-like quality of the rear light units is seen here alongside the traditional M5 badge. BMW

MIDDLE LEFT: **This time, the M5 side badges were carried on the gills let into the front wings. As is clear from this shot, they were air outlets rather than air intakes.** BMW

MIDDLE RIGHT: **The special M5 door mirrors had black lower sections and followed the trend of incorporating a repeater for the turn indicator.** BMW

BOTTOM RIGHT: **The ventilated and cross-drilled brake disc is clear in this picture, behind the M Radial Spoke wheel of an E60 M5.** BMW

■ THE E60 AND E61 V10 MODELS

During the E39 period, many of the cosmetic features of the M5 had been available at extra cost as M Sport accessories for the more mainstream models. No doubt customer feedback from those who had bought the real thing discouraged BMW from doing the same again, and the E60 M5 was very carefully distinguished from other E60 models. At the front end, there was a completely unique design with large air intakes in the apron where other models had fog lights, and wider front wings were fitted, with decorative air intakes that displayed M5 badges.

The M5 was also given flared sill panels and distinctive door-mirror bodies with blacked-out lower sections. At the rear, a body-colour spoiler on the boot lid was normally fitted, but could be deleted on request. A special rear apron incorporated a diffuser panel in the centre and flaps that wrapped over each of the four exhaust tailpipes, while the area around the number-plate recess was subtly different from the mainstream E60 design.

Wheels were a special design for the M5. Both E60 saloon and E61 Touring models came with a 19-inch size M Radial Spoke type, with 8.5-inch front rims but 9.5-inch rear rims with wider tyres. These cast alloy wheels were also known as Style 166M types, and a Style 167M was available as an alternative in some markets. These alternative wheels were forged and polished alloys similar in style to those used on the E63 M6 coupé and the E64 M6 convertible, and again had wider rims for the rear wheels. Both wheel styles came with conventional tyres rather than the run-flat types that were standard on the mainstream E60 and E61 models.

THE S85 V10 ENGINE

The S62 V8 engine was going to be a hard act to follow. For the next M5, BMW obviously needed an engine with more power and torque than before in order to give better performance. However, an increasingly important concern throughout the motor industry was to reduce fuel consumption and exhaust emissions. An engine of larger capacity than the 5-litre S62 would send out the wrong message to BMW's customers in general, even though M5 enthusiasts might not have cared.

So the decision was to make the new engine another 5-litre type, but to make it different from before by building a V10 design. For marketing purposes, it would tie in nicely with the V10 engine that had been BMW's Formula 1 engine in the Williams cars after 2000. Meanwhile, the costs of this new design would be spread by sharing the engine with the planned new M6 model, and by making it the basis of a V8 that used the same architecture and would power the next-generation M3.

Although the V10 racing engine might be part of the inspiration, it was not going to be suitable as the basis of a new road-car engine. So the job of designing the new engine family was entrusted to BMW engineer Thomas Shears. The new V10 would make the new E60-based car the first M5 to have an engine that was not derived from any production design.

The engine was designated an S85 type and specifically an S85 B50 in 5-litre form. Shears and his team drew it up around a cast aluminium-silicon alloy cylinder block with a 90-degree angle between the cylinder banks. The block was a bed plate design that was split at the crankshaft axis. The five-bearing crankshaft was forged from steel and was an interesting design with shared crankpins that gave uneven firing intervals of 90 or 54 degrees; counterweights were used to ensure smooth running. The firing order was 1-6-5-10-2-7-3-8-4-9.

The cylinder heads were also cast from aluminium, and of course carried four valves for each of the ten cylinders. In line with existing Motorsport practice, there were four separate camshafts to actuate those valves, and each one had its own VANOS system. For absolute reliability, the inlet camshafts were driven by a chain while the exhaust camshafts depended on a gear drive. Forged aluminium pistons came from the Motorsport division of Mahle, gave a very high 12:1 compression ratio and were cooled by oil. There were ten individual electronically controlled throttle butterflies and a semi-dry-sump lubrication system where the primary pump and recirculating pump were supplemented by a scavenging pump for each cylinder bank to ensure ample lubrication under extreme cornering or braking forces.

The powerful MSS 65 engine management system that controlled all these functions had been developed by the M division in conjunction with their colleagues responsible for the Williams Formula 1 engine, and used three 32-bit microprocessors (three times as many as on the V8 engine in the E39 M5). It was capable of 200 million operations per second. It received input 200 times a second about the position of the accelerator pedal from two contactless potentiometers, and was capable of fully opening or closing the ten throttle butterflies in just 120 milliseconds. The MSS 65 also pioneered a new 'ionic current' misfire and engine

THE E60 AND E61 V10 MODELS

The quad-cam V10 engine was another hugely complicated piece of engineering. In these two pictures, the 90-degree angle between the cylinder banks is clear. It was chosen to suit a V8 derivative for the M3 models as well. BMW

■ THE E60 AND E61 V10 MODELS

ABOVE: **The exhausts of the S85 V10 engine glow red-hot as it is put through strenuous testing on the dynamometer.** BMW

LEFT: **As usual, BMW took great care over the presentation of the M5's engine. The 'M V10' identification was unmistakable, but the engine was so complex that few owners would ever dare to peer under that plastic top cover.** BMW

THE E60 AND E61 V10 MODELS

BMW AND THE V10 FORMULA 1 ENGINE

After a ten-year absence from Formula 1 racing, BMW returned for the 1998 season as engine supplier to the Williams team. BMW created a new V10 engine for the Williams FW22 car, which made its racing début in 2000. However, the Williams team never became fully competitive with the Ferrari team (then with Michael Schumacher as lead driver), and BMW decided to end its agreement with Williams in 2005.

In the early 2000s, the FIA required engines of no more than 3 litres' capacity, and all versions of the BMW V10 had 2998cc. The first one was called the E41, and had a 72-degree angle between cylinder banks; the design then progressed through iterations called P81 (2001), P82 (2002), P83 (2003), P84 (2004) and P85 (2005). The first V10 developed 750PS at 14,000rpm, and the final version developed around 950PS.

Having severed its relationship with Williams, in June 2005 BMW bought the private Swiss team Sauber outright to continue its Formula 1 activities. The FIA then required all teams to use 2.4-litre V8 engines for the 2006 season, and BMW built no more V10s.

RIGHT: **It was the BMW V10 Formula 1 engines that provided inspiration for the S85 engine in the M5. This is the one that was used in the Williams FW27 car.** MAGGOT666PL/WIKIMEDIA

This was the Williams FW27 car, seen here driven by Nick Heidfeld in the 2005 Canadian Grand Prix. TMWOLF/WIKIMEDIA

113

■ THE E60 AND E61 V10 MODELS

For those who really wanted to know, BMW made available this picture of the V10's internals. Note the complex drive for the four camshafts, the inner pair being driven by chain and the outer pair by gears. BMW

knock detection system. This worked by passing a low voltage across the spark plugs immediately after the ignition spark, and fed back to the management system.

The redline of 8,250rpm was astonishingly high for such a complex engine. As put into production, the new 5-litre V10 delivered 500PS (493bhp) at a high 7,750rpm with torque of 520Nm (384lb ft) at 6,100rpm. Although it weighed only 1kg (2.2lb) more than the 5-litre S62 V8, it developed 100PS more. Overall, the S85 engine was a stupendous achievement, and it swept the board at the 2005 International Engine of the Year contest with wins in no fewer than four categories: International Engine of the Year, Best Performance Engine, Best New Engine and Best Engine above 4.0 litres. It very nearly repeated that feat in the 2006 contest, claiming three awards and missing out for obvious reasons in the Best New Engine category. And that was not the end of it: in 2007, it won the Best Performance Engine and Best Engine above 4.0 litres categories, and then in 2008 won the Best Engine above 4.0 litres category yet again.

None of that international acclaim stopped it from being somewhat controversial among M5 enthusiasts, however!

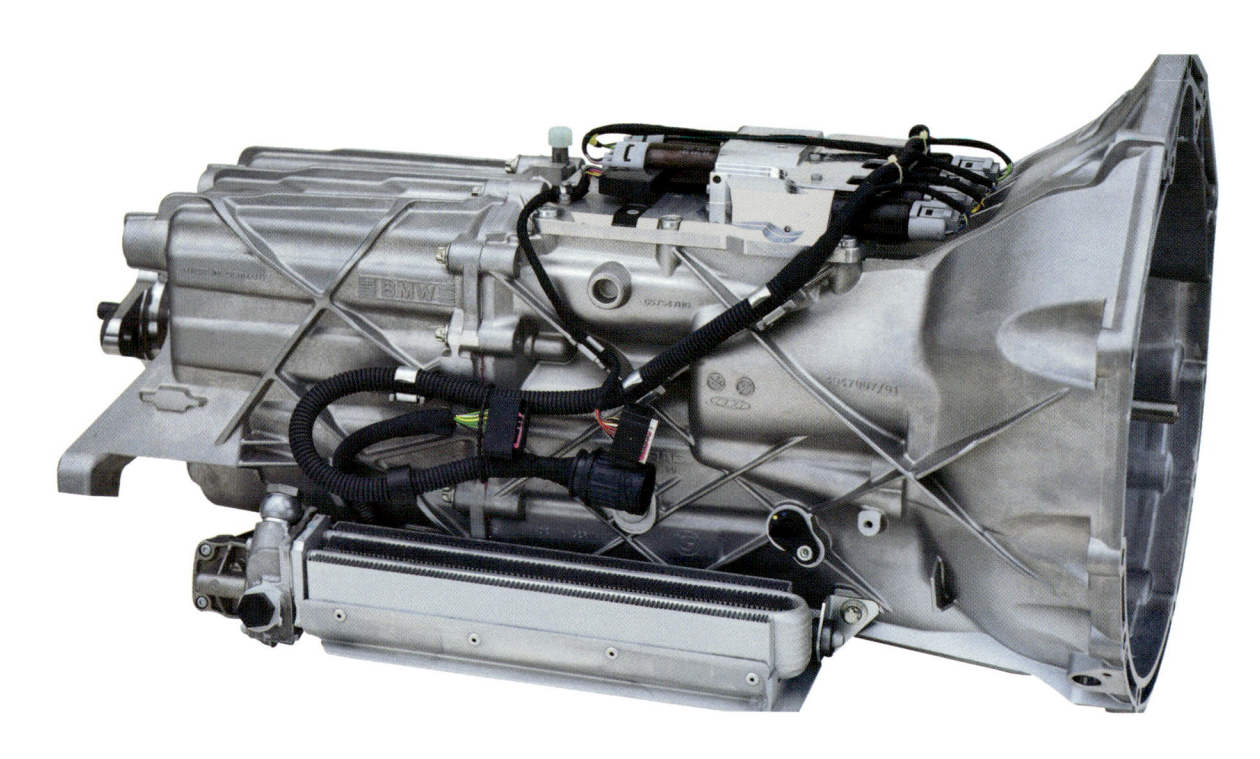

The Sequential Manual Gearbox was used for the first time on an M5. Here it is, with the standard transmission fluid cooler in the foreground at the bottom. BMW

THE E60 AND E61 V10 MODELS

THE SMG GEARBOX

All the earlier M5s – E28, E34 and E39 alike – had been available only with conventional manual gearboxes, although in each case these had been advanced for their time, typically with one more gear than mainstream gearboxes of the day. However, on its smaller M3 models, BMW had for some time been using a gearbox that combined the best features of manual and automatic transmissions. This was the SMG (Sequential Manual Gearbox), and for the E60 and E61 models the company decided to make the latest iteration of this design standard.

Although the design principles of the SMG III gearbox were the same as those of earlier SMG types, this third one to carry the name was the first to be designed from the ground up as an SMG type rather than adapted from an existing manual gearbox. Like its predecessors, it gave the driver two-pedal control, providing a choice between fully automatic and manual gear selection modes. The SMG III, however, boasted seven forward speeds, one more than earlier versions.

In automatic mode, it was capable of lightning-fast gear-changes, claimed to be 20 per cent faster than those of the earlier SMG II in the E46 M3 models; the actual time quoted was 65 milliseconds. It came with eleven driver-selectable Drivelogic programmes, five operational in automatic mode and six in manual mode, and a number of other features such as a hill holder and a downshift assist that would briefly dip the clutch to prevent wheel spin.

It also brought to the M5 for the first time a feature called Launch Control that had been pioneered on the E46 M3. Launch Control linked the car's electronic control systems to provide the fastest possible acceleration from rest (and was not recommended for use on public roads!). Once all the necessary settings were in place, the driver floored the accelerator until the engine revs reached a governed 4,000rpm and then moved the gear lever, whereupon the car took off like a rocket and the SMG performed all the necessary gear-changes seamlessly.

SUSPENSION, STEERING AND BRAKES

The all-aluminium suspension of the mainstream E60 and E61 models with its MacPherson struts at the front and multi-link design at the rear was already advanced, but BMW M took it further for the M5 models.

At the front, the track was widened by 23mm (0.9in), and thicker anti-roll bars were added to both saloon and Tour-

---

THE SEQUENTIAL MANUAL GEARBOX

BMW introduced its Sequential Manual Gearbox as an extra-cost option on the E36 M3 models in March 1997, after announcing this new development in July 1996. Although the M3 had traditionally been supplied with a manual gearbox, there was persistent demand for an automatic option, especially in North America. So BMW M developed the SMG as a gearbox that gave the best of both worlds.

The SMG was based on established practice in motor racing, and depended on an electronic control system that actuated a servo-operated clutch. The system had a shift lever similar to that of an automatic, but with two overlapping 'gates'. Moving the lever to the left-hand gate selected the fully automatic Economy mode, but moving it to the right or Sports gate gave sequential up- or down-changes under manual control. Moving the lever forwards in that right-hand gate gave an up-change, and moving it backwards gave a down-change. In addition, there were Formula 1-style 'paddles' on the steering wheel to give the driver fingertip control of both up and down shifts. Whichever control method was used the changes were slick and fast, and the system incorporated checks and overrides to prevent damage caused by insensitive use.

The first production version of the SMG was a six-speed type, but it did not earn itself a good reputation. An improved SMG II gearbox, again with six speeds, became available in the E46 M3 during 2001. This was the first gearbox to feature Launch Control, and its control software also offered a wide range of driver-adjustable programs.

The SMG III gearbox of the E60 and E61 M5 models was the third iteration of the design, this time with seven speeds.

■ THE E60 AND E61 V10 MODELS

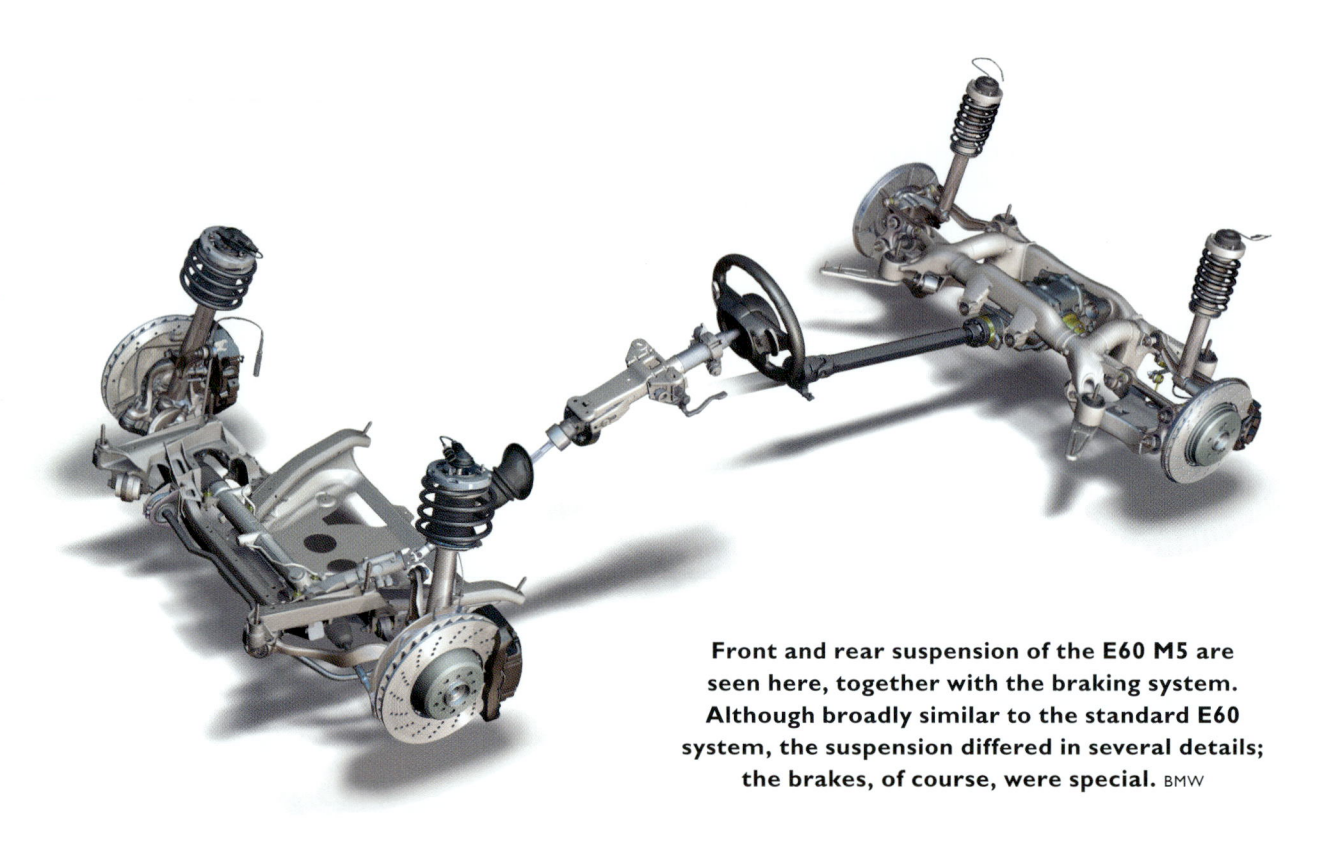

Front and rear suspension of the E60 M5 are seen here, together with the braking system. Although broadly similar to the standard E60 system, the suspension differed in several details; the brakes, of course, were special. BMW

This fascinating image shows the underpinnings of an E60 M5. Quite clear are the huge air intakes mounted low down behind the front apron. BMW

THE E60 AND E61 V10 MODELS

ing models, the Touring's bars being thicker than the saloon's. The front sub-frame and thrust plate were modified, and there were stiffer bushes with altered suspension geometry. The rear sub-frame was also modified, and there were different rear spring rates, a thicker anti-roll bar (again, thicker still on the Touring) and revised suspension links that had been adapted from those used on the Z8 roadster. Hollow half-shafts were a further unique M5 development, and an EDC (Electronic Damper Control) system was standard. When left in its standard automatic mode, this gave constant variation of the damper stiffness to suit the road conditions, but it could also be overridden by the driver to give Comfort, Normal or Sport settings.

For the first time on an M5, the E60 and E61 models came with the sharp rack-and-pinion steering system that such cars deserved. This was similar to the type standard on mainstream E60s and E61s, with a ratio that varied according to the amount of lock applied to even out driver input. On top of that, however, the M5s had the latest version of ZF's speed-dependent Servotronic power assistance. This time, the system was linked into the EDC system, and gave a greater degree of assistance when the dampers were set to Comfort mode than it did when they were in either Normal or Sport mode.

As for the brakes, all four wheels now came with larger discs than on any earlier M5. These were not only ventilated but also cross-drilled, and all four discs were also of two-part aluminium and cast-iron construction for improved heat dissipation. The front calipers also had twin pistons.

Every E60 and E61 M5 was also built with a Variable M Differential Lock, which gave more satisfactory control of the locking function than a traditional self-locking differential. Jointly developed by BMW M and GKN's Viscodrive division, it sensed when there was a difference in rotational speed

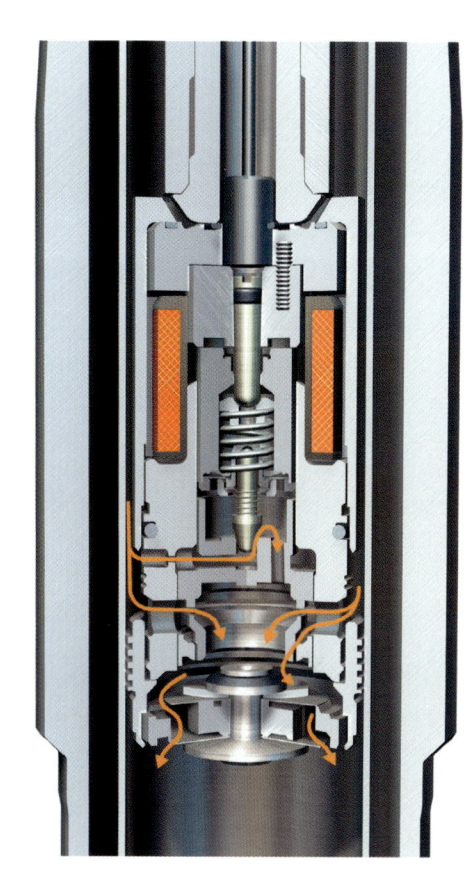

These are the EDC dampers. The sectional view on the left shows fluid flow on the upward stroke, and that on the right shows it on the downward stroke. BMW

between the two rear wheels, pressurizing a viscous silicone fluid, which in turn operated a multi-disc clutch. This then directed the drive towards the wheel with better traction.

Like the E39, the E60 and E61 cars came as standard with a Dynamic Stability Control traction control system. This version of DSC could be switched off altogether, or alternatively put into what was called M Dynamic Mode, which simply raised the threshold speed at which it operated. It also incorporated several new features, made possible by electronics and developed in a joint programme between BMW and the Teves company. Start-Off Assistant detected when the car was facing uphill and held the brakes on for a second after the driver's foot was removed from the brake, to give a hill-hold function. Brake Standby detected when the driver lifted off the accelerator abruptly, and prepared for hard braking by moving the pads closer to the rotors to give maximum braking as rapidly as pos-sible if the brake pedal was depressed. Then there was Brake Drying, which

117

■ THE E60 AND E61 V10 MODELS

depended on a rain sensor; when it detected moisture, it moved the pads to brush the discs in order to prevent water getting between them and reducing braking power.

CUSTOMIZING THE DRIVING EXPERIENCE

BMW was well aware that offering multiple variations of its cars through paint, upholstery and equipment options enabled buyers to tailor their cars to their individual tastes. From the early 1990s, the company had also offered a custom-finishing programme called BMW Individual, which further multiplied the options available within certain set limits. As a further extension of this philosophy, the company developed a number of electronic systems that enabled drivers to tailor the driving experience to suit their mood.

The M5 versions of the E60 and E61 were among the first M cars to have M Drive as standard equipment. This allowed the driver to customize aspects of the driving experience through a menu system, and it comprised the Drivelogic control system of the SMG (giving eleven choices), the throttle response speed, suspension damping and DSC activation (three choices each), and the engine power output and Servotronic steering response (two choices each). The settings could be varied at will through the iDrive system and those chosen could all be introduced together with a single press of the M button located on the steering wheel. Additional customization was available with some of the extra-cost options, such as the active front seats and the head-up display, which are explained later.

The option that perhaps appealed most to M5 enthusiasts was the ability to select three different power settings for the engine. Although there were just two overall power settings, a third setting gave faster accelerator response with the maximum power option. The least aggressive setting was P400, where engine power was limited to 400PS and the standard accelerator response mode was in place. Next up came the P500 setting, selected through the iDrive menu, which gave access to the full 500PS of the engine and also gave a more rapid accelerator response programme. Finally there was the P500 Sport setting, which gave even more rapid accelerator response. The 400PS mode was the default setting, and gave quite enough performance for most circumstances. P500 and P500 Sport were selected through the iDrive menu, and once one had been programmed in, it was available instantly at a touch of the M button on the steering wheel.

With wood trim and perforated leather, the interior of an E60 M5 had plenty of luxury appeal. Only the vertical door handles strike a rather jarring note. BMW

THE E60 AND E61 V10 MODELS

This is a later (LCI) right-hand-drive E60 M5 for the UK market, this time with the sports seats. Note how the centre console mirrors the layout on the left-hand-drive car. Those odd vertical door pulls have, fortunately, gone. HATSUKARI715/WIKIMEDIA

ON THE INSIDE

As was customary by this stage, those who entered an M5 were greeted by door sill plates that carried the M5 logo. Two different types of front seat could be had, the standard type having electrically adjustable side bolsters and the optional M Multifunction sport seats having electrically adjustable upper bolsters and 'active' headrests and lower side bolsters. The bolsters automatically inflated to improve support when they detected lateral loads (as in hard cornering). Both types of seat came with heating as standard.

There was the usual raft of upholstery options, all of them using leather and all of them accompanied by an Anthracite headlining in cloth or, to choice, Alcantara. There were also three choices of interior trim that were unique to the M5 – Brushed Aluminum Shadow, Madeira Walnut wood and Natural Olive Ash wood.

The three upholstery choices were Extended Merino Leather, Complete Merino Leather and Complete Merino Perforated Leather. The Extended option brought leather for the door panels and the door and centre armrests as

That odd-shaped box on the centre console could be used to store a mobile phone in a special release cradle. Note how the iDrive rotary control differs on this car. BMW

The shift lever for the SMG gearbox had an illuminated gear indicator in its top surface. BMW

119

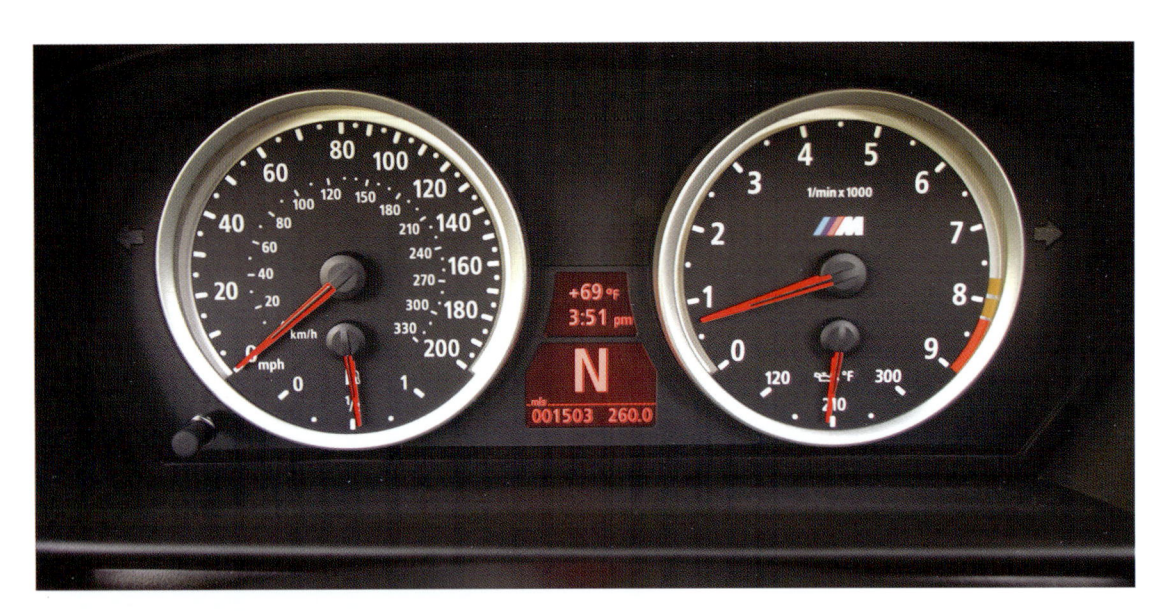

■ THE E60 AND E61 V10 MODELS

These were the dials of an E60 (or E61) M5. Red needles, aluminium 'tunnels' and the M logo on the rev counter were all to be expected. BMW

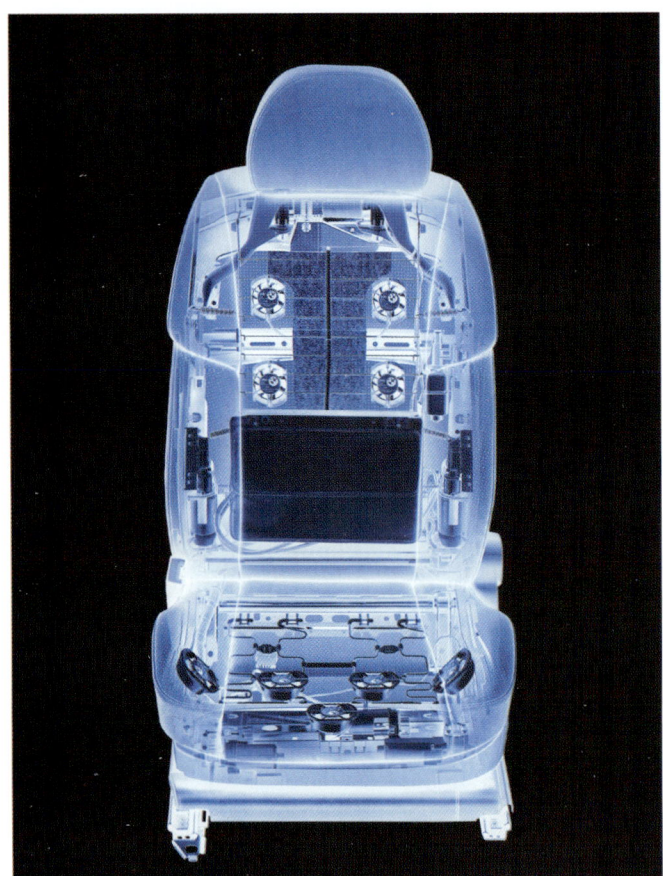

The HUD (Head-Up Display) was a new feature for the E60 and E61 models of the M5. BMW

The optional multi-function seats had a range of functions that made them complex pieces of engineering – almost too good to sit on! This cutaway view shows much of the machinery hidden away on the inside. BMW

well as the seats. With Complete Merino Leather, there was also leather on the dashboard top and bottom sections, the upper and lower door panels and the centre console. Leather coverage was the same with the perforated leather option, which had perforations on the wearing surfaces of the front seats and came as part of the ventilated seat package, which featured cooling fans in the seats themselves. This third option was available in fewer colours than the others.

For the driver, BMW M had come up with the expected selection of delights. The instrument pack was based on that used in the 545i, but the dials had aluminium bezels, red needles and white lighting, and of course the rev counter incorporated an oil temperature gauge, and the speedometer read to 330km/h or 200mph. Optional at extra cost was a head-up display that projected the vehicle's speed, the engine speed and the SMG gear setting onto the windscreen ahead of the driver. The steering wheel was a three-spoke type with a 381mm (15in) diameter that featured M tricolour stitching on the rim, racing-style gearshift paddles to operate the SMG in manual mode, and an M button on the right-hand spoke that selected the programmable M Drive mode. There was a special M Design driver's footrest, and the console around the shift lever for the SMG had a group of buttons for the Power mode, the EDC mode, the DSC system and the Drivelogic options.

THE M5 TOURING

A Touring estate model had been available alongside every BMW 5 Series saloon since the E34 range had been introduced in 1988. There was, then, inevitably a Touring derivative of the E60 range, although its separate designation of E61 reflected changes within BMW design that allowed related projects to develop with greater individuality than before.

There had been no M5 derivative of the E39 Touring, although one had been prepared, as Chapter 5 explains. It seems highly likely that no M5 derivative of the E61 range was planned in the beginning, either, because only the saloon was introduced in 2004. However, rival manufacturers were successfully selling high-performance estate cars, and BMW probably decided that it needed to be represented in that sector of the market even if it did not expect sales to be very great. So an E61 M5 Touring came to the party late, being announced nearly three years after the saloon, at the March 2007 Geneva Motor Show.

In reality, sales of the E61 M5 Touring probably conformed to BMW's expectations. Touring models had accounted for only 23 per cent of sales of the 3.8-litre E34 M5, and the absence of a Touring from the E39 M5 line-up suggests that BMW thought this was not a large enough quantity to continue with a new Touring. The figures for the E61 variant were even poorer. Even though right-hand-drive cars were made available this time around, the grand total of 1,025 cars was achieved only after the production run had been extended into 2010 to finish four months after M5 saloon production had ended. The top three markets for the car were Germany (where 302 were sold), Great Britain and Ireland (208) and Italy (184). So, realistically, the E61 M5 Touring was largely a flag-waving exercise by BMW.

None of that made the car any less exciting than its saloon equivalent. The drivetrain of the two cars was exactly the same, and the equipment and options were exactly the same as well. There were a few necessary differences, such as fatter anti-roll bars front and rear to cope with the greater weight of the Touring (especially when laden), but there was never any hint that the more practical Touring was any slower than the contemporary M5 saloon. It was very much a case of horses for courses – although in this case, not very many buyers were interested in the course that the M5 Touring ran on.

PRODUCTION CHANGES

Production changes are never welcome, and BMW avoided them as much as possible in the early years of E60 and E61 M5 production. Although the paint options were broadened in May 2005 with a range of colours from BMW Individual and one new colour exclusive to BMW M, the first substantial change arrived with the 2006 models in September 2005. This brought a transponder key in place of the traditional ignition key, with an engine Start/Stop button on the dashboard. A further minor change during that season was the addition of an auxiliary input (for MP3 players and the like) to the ICE system in March 2006.

There were more minor changes for the 2007 cars from September 2006, when an HD radio option became available and the satellite navigation system was improved. More major changes were made for North America, where a Tire Pressure Monitor that used sensors on the wheels replaced the Flat Tyre Monitor system, and a six-speed manual gearbox became standard. This manual gearbox was never made available outside Canada and the USA.

Like the other E60 and E61 models, the M5s were then more extensively revised in March 2007, and the later cars are usually known by the BMW term LCI types. (The letters stand for Life Cycle Impulse, which is BMW's politically correct way of describing a mid-life makeover.) Under the skin, the most important changes were to the SMG, which was reprogrammed and gained an uprated hydraulic pump.

Key exterior changes were to the lights. The headlights gained an adaptive cornering function, and LED turn indicators arrived. Daytime running lights were standardized at the front. LED tail lights were also introduced, characterized by horizontal lines behind the lenses. The design of the front spoiler and the front wheel lips both changed, and

■ THE E60 AND E61 V10 MODELS

*It was quite surprising how much difference the trim chosen could make to the interior ambience. This is an **LCI** model with sports seats, and the **Brushed Aluminum Shadow** trim instead of the wood type seen on the other cars pictured in this chapter.* BMW

there were some changes to the paint colour options. Inside the passenger cabin came new trim materials, larger head restraints, and new designs for the centre console and door trim panels, where the hand grip was deleted and the mirror and window controls were repositioned. A six-disc CD changer was added to the dashboard, and the iDrive system gained programmable memory buttons.

New options were introduced at the same time. These included soft-close doors, a heated steering wheel, an iPod/USB adapter for the ICE system and, from the BMW Individual range, a new sixteen-speaker Premium sound system. Also new but not available in all markets were twenty-way Comfort front seats, based on those available in other E60 models but distinguished by active upper bolsters. These invariably came with seat ventilation and perforated Merino leather.

More changes were made to options over the next couple of years. High Beam Assistant (an automatic headlamp dimming system) became available on 2008 models from September 2007. For 2009, September 2008 introduced more paint colour changes and a modified iDrive controller with fixed buttons. The last changes then entered production in March 2009. All models gained larger door mirrors, an iDrive 2.0 with a hard-drive satellite navigation system, a larger

WHAT THE PRESS THOUGHT

Bimmer, April 2006

'The polarising look of the latest 5 Series is mitigated only slightly by its M-specific bodywork.'

'Our time in this car made a profound impression. We emerged from the experience totally infatuated, eagerly awaiting our next opportunity to further explore the M5's oh-so-seductive personality and performance. If there's a better sedan on the market, we haven't driven it.'

'The M5 is truly, outrageously fast … [and] it has the grip and the braking to go with it.'

'The 5.0-liter V10 … likes to rev, even though it isn't very torquey relative to its horsepower output … in terms of character, [it's] an engine that's powerful and high-revving without being explosive in its delivery.'

'Plant your right foot to the floor and speed builds with amazing rapidity and very little drama.'

'Our only real complaint centred on the M5's SMG transmission, which on the track as well as the street seemed to shift too slowly in even the fastest of its five modes.'

Top Gear
(The car tested was an E60 saloon.)

'It's a world of motoring perfection. If you want to take it on … don't bother. It doesn't matter what you've got. It doesn't matter what you've ever driven. This is quicker, it's faster, it's MORE astonishing. You just can't believe you're in a big 4-door saloon because it goes and it feels and it SOUNDS like a Ferrari 430, and that's about the best car I've ever driven. The steering, the brakes, the power. And this noise … The driving experience just dominates everything … It's an epic car, just brilliant.'

Top Gear, June 2007
(The car tested was an E61 Touring.)

'Grip levels remain good in the Touring, but the single most impressive thing about it is that you don't notice it's an estate. It doesn't feel like there's any extra weight hung out back, and there's no more wind noise than with the saloon version.'

'The simple truth is that the M5 isn't suited to Britain. The engine really starts to wake up above 5,000rpm, but in all but the first two gears, you're in danger of losing your driving licence.'

Evo, April 2008

'The BMW requires a ritual (press starter button, select "Power", dial up the middle setting for the EDC dampers) and some skill before it reveals its talents. Too much aggression leads to jumpy progress, the traction control frantically dealing with your clumsy inputs, and the engine's highly strung nature means it punishes binary inputs to the throttle.'

'The engine itself is an awesome device. There's strong, insistent torque between 2,500 and 4,500rpm, but the big power needs to be sought out. Keep the throttle pinned and the delivery gets more intense past 5,000rpm and then switches to full-on lunacy in the final rush between 6,500 and 8,500rpm.'

Performance Car, February 2009

'The marketing men have got heavily involved with the car's inception and have probably made it a little bit too complex for its own good. You don't need all those different modes, and I should imagine that, like us, most owners will drive the car in one or two different setups and ignore the rest.'

■ THE E60 AND E61 V10 MODELS

screen and improved 3D graphics. Some European models were also given BMW Connected Drive internet capability, and some were also fitted with the BMW Efficient Dynamics brake energy regeneration system, but these items were not made available on the North American NB93 models.

THE RHD CARS

The M models had been consistently popular in right-hand-drive markets such as Great Britain and Australia, and there was never any question that the E60 M5 should be built only with left-hand drive. Indeed, when BMW came to prepare the E61 M5 Touring, a right-hand-drive version was included in the production plans because it was going to help boost production volumes. Rather less than 25 per cent of those made in fact had right-hand drive.

Figures from BMW show that Great Britain and Ireland combined took 1,776 of the fourth-generation M5 cars, or nearly 46 per cent of right-hand-drive production. Australia came second with the much smaller total of 339 cars. In the UK, the E60 and E61 M5s became available from May 2005.

As with earlier versions of the M5, Japan took its M5s with left-hand drive even though right-hand drive was the national standard. This was to suit the Japanese perception that left-hand-drive cars had additional status. (For the record, 1,357 examples of the fourth-generation M5 were sold in Japan.)

THE NORTH AMERICAN CARS

The E61 Touring version of the M5 was never made available in North America, and both Canada and the USA had to be content with the E60 saloon version. Its specification was essentially the same as that of the European cars, but all cars came with the M Radial Spoke alloys, and the alterna-

This is a North American E60 M5. BMW had made it as close to the European version as they could, but a careful look here will reveal the amber side marker lights under the clear covers of the front light units. BMW

THE E60 AND E61 V10 MODELS

complaints that its low-speed changes were rougher than those of a conventional automatic. There was also a groundswell of feeling that a car with the performance and character of the M5 ought to have a conventional manual gearbox. As a result, the North American dealers put a degree of pressure on BMW to come up with such a transmission for the M5. BMW did exactly that, and in September 2006 began production of a special version for the USA and Canada only that had a six-speed manual gearbox.

The gearbox chosen was a ZF Type G, and it was made available as the standard gearbox from October 2006, the SMG being re-listed as an option. There was no significant difference in performance between the two versions of the M5, although some tests did show the manual-gearbox car to be slightly slower in some conditions because the DSC (Dynamic Stability Control) would intervene to prevent wheelspin by cutting power. So for the 2008 model-year, cars were fitted with a disabling switch for the DSC, and a service modification allowed earlier cars to be modified to the same standard. Cars with the manual gearbox that also had the optional head-up display did not show the gear selected on the windscreen ahead of the driver.

There were 9,491 E60 M5 saloons built for North America between 2005 and 2009. Of these, 8,800 were delivered to US customers and the remaining 691 found buyers in Canada. Figures currently available show that only 1,364 cars were built with the six-speed manual gearbox, and that total included six pre-production models. So, despite the concerns of North American dealers, their customers remained content on the whole to take their M5s with the SMG III gearbox.

Only on the North American cars was it possible to order a six-speed manual gearbox. This is what the option looked like from the driver's seat. UNITY MEDIA

SPECIAL EDITIONS

BMW built only one special edition of its fourth-generation M5, and that was introduced at the end of 2009 as part of the celebrations associated with the twenty-fifth anniversary of the M5 range. Both E60 saloon and E61 Touring versions were available.

The 25th Anniversary M5

The 25th Anniversary M5 cars were built in late November and early December 2009, and there were twenty-seven in all. Just three of these were Touring models, of which two

tive Style 167M wheels were not available. As always, North American cars came with amber side marker lights, the front ones being integrated into the headlight units.

Perhaps the biggest disappointment for North American customers was that the impressive Launch Control feature had been tamed. Where European models would 'launch' at 4,000rpm, the North American version of the system kept the launch engine speed right down to 1,500rpm, and at higher engine speeds the driver was required to take charge of the gear-changes.

Some North American customers were not very impressed by the SMG gearbox, and BMW received some

THE E60 AND E61 V10 MODELS

were sold in Germany and one in Switzerland. Of the twenty-four saloons, thirteen had left-hand drive, of which eight went to Germany and five to Brazil. The remaining eleven cars were right-hand-drive saloons, of which one went to Australia and the other ten were sold in Great Britain.

All these cars had Frozen Gray paint from the BMW Individual range, and were to some extent intended to showcase the availability of these new finishes. The 'Frozen' options had a fashionable matt finish, achieved by applying a BMW-developed silk matt clear coat over the coloured metallic base coat. BMW claimed that they met or exceeded all its standards for durability and longevity, although they did come with certain conditions, and the standard factory warranty was subject to strict observation of these. Traditional polishing was strictly forbidden, and all surface contaminants had to be removed quickly and carefully in case they left glossy patches on the paint. (Note that the company's English-language publicity material also usually described them as 'matte' finishes, as BMW had standardized on American English spellings; a further example was the use of Gray in the colour name rather than the preferred British English 'grey'.)

For most of the 25th Anniversary M5 cars, there was a choice of two special upholstery options, again drawn from the BMW Individual range. The choices were Black complete Merino leather and two-tone ('Bi-Color') Black and Silverstone complete Merino leather, in each case with Light Gray contrast stitching. Neither of these was offered on the UK cars, however, which instead came with standard Black complete Merino leather.

The famous Ring Taxi was also presented in full warpaint, although not in the traditional style of BMW's works racers. BMW

THE E60 AND E61 V10 MODELS

WHAT MIGHT HAVE BEEN – THE M5 CSL

In the second half of 2003, a few months before the E60 M5 made its debut, BMW introduced a very special limited edition of the M3 coupé called the M3 CSL. Those initials came from the legendary 1971 homologation special based on the big 3.0 CS coupé. The initials then, as again in 2003, stood for 'Coupé Sport Leicht' (lightweight sports coupé), and the M3 CSL was created as a lightweight track model, employing several elements made from GFP and featuring a higher engine tune than the standard M3. (GFP stands for the German words 'glasfaserverstärktes Polyester' or carbon-fibre-reinforced polyester, and is a high-tech lightweight material.)

Could there really have been a racing M5? BMW allowed enthusiasts to think so when they painted their one-off CSL model in the traditional M Power colours and issued pictures of it on the track. BMW

The concept was tried on the M5 as well, and a single prototype M5 CSL was revealed in public at the time of the M5's 25th Anniversary celebrations in 2010. The car was clearly a feasibility prototype, even though it was presented with M tricolour racing stripes. Its key elements were light weight and a more powerful version of the V10 engine. BMW claimed that it was 50kg (110lb) lighter than a standard E60 M5, thanks partly to a carbon-fibre roof panel and a stripped-out interior with no rear seat and a pair of lightweight carbon-fibre racing seats in the front.

The engine had been enlarged to 5.5 litres with a longer stroke, and featured a carbon-fibre manifold with a larger capacity air box and a secondary oil cooler. The additional oil cooler drew cold air through an additional duct in the front apron. BMW would not be drawn on precise power and torque figures, but when the car was shown to journalists in 2010, BMW M's development chief Albert Biermann hinted that the power output was around 580PS and the torque around 500Nm (close to 400lb ft).

The M5 CSL had an uprated version of the seven-speed M Double Clutch Transmission used in the M3. Its suspension was little altered from standard, featuring only different mapping for the variable dampers. As for performance, BMW again refused to be drawn, but Biermann told Greg Kable of *Autocar* that it was 'comfortably faster the standard M5's 4.1sec 0–100km/h'. The company did, however, claim that the M5 CSL was twenty seconds faster than a standard E60 M5 around the Nürburgring.

It is not clear why the car was not taken forward to production, but perhaps BMW could see no convenient racing category where the lightweight M5 could be used.

127

PRODUCTION TOTALS FOR THE E60 AND E61 M5

There were 20,589 examples of the E60 and E61 M5.

Type	Build dates	Total
NB91	September 2004–December 2009	6,427
NB92	March 2005–December 2009	3,646
NB93	September 2005–December 2009	9,491
	(Sub-total)	19,564
PV91	March 2007–April 2010	803
PV92	March 2007–February 2010	222
	(Sub-total)	1,025
	Grand total	**20,589**

Notes:
NB91 cars were European-specification LHD saloons
NB92 cars were European-specification RHD saloons
NB93 cars were North American-specification LHD saloons
PV91 cars were European-specification LHD Touring estates
PV92 cars were European-specification RHD Touring estates

PERFORMANCE FIGURES FOR E60 AND E61 M5 MODELS

European models 0–60mph 4.8 sec
Maximum 250km/h (155mph), electronically limited

Although BMW quoted 4.7 seconds for the 0–100km/h (0–62mph) time when the cars were first introduced, several road tests improved on that. Even in the USA, where the Launch Control was inhibited to a degree, *Motor Trend* magazine found that an M5 saloon could hit 60mph from rest in 4.5 seconds. The figure used by BMW M development chief Albert Biermann in 2010 to Greg Kable of *Autocar* was 4.1 seconds for the 0–100km/h (0–62mph) time.

BMW also claimed that the E60 M5 could reach 330km/h (205mph) with the speed limiter disabled – which at least justified the figures on the optimistic-looking speedometer.

INTERIOR TRIM OPTIONS

Names are shown in their English forms throughout.

September 2004 to April 2005

There were initially just three interior trim options available, all of them exclusive to BMW M.

Type	Code	Type	Code
Brushed Aluminum Shadow	737	Natural Olive Ash	4MK
Chestnut Brown Madeira Walnut	4ME		

May 2005 to April 2010

In May 2005, the existing three options were supplemented by three more taken from the BMW Individual catalogue to make six options in all. Note that the BMW Individual options were not available in every country where the M5 was sold.

Type	Code	Type	Code
Amarone Walnut	XE1	Figured Red Brown Eucalyptus	XE3
Brushed Aluminum Shadow	737	Natural Olive Ash	4MK
Chestnut Brown Madeira Walnut	4ME	Piano Black	XE7

THE E60 AND E61 V10 MODELS

E60 AND E61 M5 SPECIFICATIONS

Engine:
Type S85 B50 V10-cylinder petrol
4999cc (92mm x 75.2mm)
Four overhead camshafts, with chain drive for inlet camshafts and gearwheel drive for exhaust camshafts; Double-VANOS variable camshaft timing
Four valves per cylinder
Five-bearing crankshaft
Compression ratio 12.0:1
Siemens MSS65 engine management system
Exhaust with dual catalytic converters
507PS (500bhp) at 7,750rpm
520Nm (383lb ft) at 6,100rpm

Transmission:
Seven-speed SMG III Sequential M gearbox
    Ratios 3.99:1, 2.65:1, 1.81:1, 1.39:1, 1.16:1, 1.00:1, 0.83:1
Six-speed ZF Type G manual gearbox available on North American models from September 2006
    Ratios 4.05:1, 2.40:1, 1.58:1, 1.19:1, 1.00:1, 0.87:1

Axle ratio:
3.62:1 (all types)
(Variable M Differential Lock standard on all models)

Suspension, steering and brakes:
Front suspension with MacPherson struts, coil springs, gas dampers and 26.5mm anti-roll bar (28mm on E61 Touring)
Multi-link rear suspension with coil springs, gas dampers and 18mm anti-roll bar (20mm on E61 Touring)
Rack-and-pinion steering with lock-dependent ratio (mean ratio 12.4:1) and standard ZF Servotronic speed-variable power assistance
Disc brakes all round, 374mm (14.7in) ventilated and cross-drilled on front wheels and 370mm (14.56in) ventilated and cross-drilled on rear wheels; 'floating' two-piece discs on all four wheels; twin-piston front calipers; twin hydraulic circuits; ABS standard

Dimensions:
Overall length:	4,855mm (191.2in)	Overall height:	1,469mm (57.8in) – saloon
	4,864mm (191.5in) from 2008		1,512mm (59.5in) – Touring
Overall width:	1,846mm (72.7in)	Wheelbase:	2,889mm (113.7in) – saloon
			2,880mm (113.4in) – Touring

Wheels and tyres:
8.5J x 19 five-stud alloy front wheels with 255/40ZR19 tyres
9.5J x 19 five-stud alloy rear wheels with 285/35ZR19 tyres (E60 saloon) or 275/35ZR19 tyres (E61 Touring)

Kerb weights:
Saloon   1,855kg (4,090lb)
Touring   1,955kg (4,310lb)

PAINT OPTIONS

Names are shown in their English forms throughout.

September 2004 to April 2005

There were seven paint colours available in this period.

Colour	Code	Colour	Code
Alpine White III	300	Sepang Bronze metallic	A32
Black Sapphire metallic	475	Silver Gray metallic	A08
Indianapolis Red metallic	A31	Silverstone II metallic	A29
Interlagos Blue metallic	A30		

May 2005 to August 2005

A further eight colours, of which seven were from the BMW Individual range, were added in May 2005. This gave a choice of fifteen colours. Carbon Black metallic was available only through the BMW Individual programme (at extra cost) in this period.

Colour	Code	Colour	Code
Alpine White III	300	Indianapolis Red metallic	A31
Black Opal metallic	S12	Interlagos Blue metallic	A30
Black Sapphire metallic	475	Ruby Black metallic	S23/X03
Blue Onyx metallic	S11	Sepang Bronze metallic	A32
Brass metallic	FQ 95-4472	Sepia metallic	474
Carbon Black metallic	416	Silver Gray metallic	A08
Dark Malachite Green metallic	S10	Silverstone II metallic	A29
Diamond metallic	A10		

September 2005 to February 2007

Two more colours from the BMW Individual range were added to make a total of seventeen options. Carbon Black metallic was available only through the BMW Individual programme (at extra cost) in this period.

Colour	Code	Colour	Code
Alpine White III	300	Indianapolis Red metallic	A31
Azurite Black metallic	S34	Interlagos Blue metallic	A30
Black Opal metallic	S12	Moonstone metallic	S37/X04
Black Sapphire metallic	475	Ruby Black metallic	S23/X03
Blue Onyx metallic	S11	Sepang Bronze metallic	A32
Brass metallic	FQ 95-4472	Sepia metallic	474
Carbon Black metallic	416	Silver Gray metallic	A08
Dark Malachite Green metallic	S10	Silverstone II metallic	A29
Diamond metallic	A10		

March 2007 to August 2007

Six options were deleted from March 2007 and three new ones were added, leaving a choice of fourteen colours. Carbon Black metallic was available only through the BMW Individual programme (at extra cost) in this period.

Colour	Code	Colour	Code
Alpine White III	300	Interlagos Blue metallic	A30
Azurite Black metallic	S34	Monaco Blue metallic	A35
Black Sapphire metallic	475	Moonstone metallic	S37/X04
Blue Onyx metallic	S11	Ruby Black metallic	S23/X03
Carbon Black metallic	416	Sepang Bronze metallic	A32
Diopside Black metallic	S44	Silverstone II metallic	A29
Indianapolis Red metallic	A31	Space Gray metallic	A52

September 2007 to August 2008

In September 2007, one new colour was added to the existing options, making a choice of fifteen. The new colour was Aventurine Silver metallic (code S58). Carbon Black metallic was available only through the BMW Individual programme (at extra cost) until March 2008.

September 2008 to April 2010

In September 2008, one colour (Blue Onyx metallic) was deleted from the options. The remaining fourteen were available until the end of production in April 2010.

Colour	Code	Colour	Code
Alpine White III	300	Interlagos Blue metallic	A30
Aventurine Silver metallic	S58	Monaco Blue metallic	A35
Azurite Black metallic	S34	Moonstone metallic	S37/X04
Black Sapphire metallic	475	Ruby Black metallic	S23/X03
Carbon Black metallic	416	Sepang Bronze metallic	A32
Diopside Black metallic	S44	Silverstone II metallic	A29
Indianapolis Red metallic	A31	Space Gray metallic	A52

Notes:
(1) Five of the paints used were also available on other BMW models. These were Alpine White III, Black Sapphire metallic, Monaco Blue metallic, Silver Gray metallic and Space Gray metallic.
(2) Five paints were exclusive to BMW M models. These were Carbon Black metallic, Indianapolis Red metallic, Interlagos Blue metallic, Sepang Bronze metallic and Silverstone II metallic.
(3) Eleven paints were drawn from the BMW Individual range. These were Aventurine Silver metallic, Azurite Black metallic, Black Opal metallic, Blue Onyx metallic, Brass metallic, Dark Malachite Green metallic, Diamond metallic, Diopside Black metallic, Moonstone metallic, Ruby Black metallic and Sepia metallic. BMW Individual paints were not available in every country where the M5 was sold.
(4) In addition, Frozen Gray, which was used only on the 25th Anniversary Edition, was drawn from the BMW Individual range.

■ THE E60 AND E61 V10 MODELS

UPHOLSTERY OPTIONS

Names are shown in their English forms throughout.

September 2004 to April 2005

There were initially eleven upholstery options for the E60 and E61 M5 models, all of them exclusive to BMW M.

Colour	Code	Colour	Code
Black complete Merino leather	X3SW	Light Sepang Bronze extended Merino leather	LKA8
Black complete Merino leather (perforated)	X2SW	Portland Brown complete Merino leather	X3BI
Black extended Merino leather	LKSW	Silverstone II complete Merino leather	X3A9
Indianapolis Red complete Merino leather	X3A7	Silverstone II complete Merino leather (perforated)	X2A9
Light Sepang Bronze complete Merino leather	X3A8	Silverstone II extended Merino leather	LKA9
Light Sepang Bronze complete Merino leather (perforated)	X2A8		

May 2005 to March 2007

The eleven original options remained available and were supplemented by six more from May 2005 to make a total of seventeen choices. The six new options were all drawn from the BMW Individual catalogue.

Colour	Code	Colour	Code
Amarone Merino leather	8025168	Light Sepang Bronze complete Merino leather (perforated)	X2A8
Black complete Merino leather	X3SW	Light Sepang Bronze extended Merino leather	LKA8
Black complete Merino leather (perforated)	X2SW	Platinum Merino leather	8020297
Black extended Merino leather	LKSW	Polar Gray Merino leather	8025170
Caramel Merino leather	8022290	Portland Brown complete Merino leather	X3BI
Champagne Merino leather	8025169	Silverstone II complete Merino leather	X3A9
Indianapolis Red complete Merino leather	X3A7	Silverstone II complete Merino leather (perforated)	X2A9
Light Ecru Merino leather	8023282	Silverstone II extended Merino leather	LKA9
Light Sepang Bronze complete Merino leather	X3A8		

THE E60 AND E61 V10 MODELS

March 2007 to April 2010

Two options were discontinued (Caramel Merino leather and Light Ecru Merino leather) and two new ones were introduced (Rust Brown Merino leather and Syrah Blue Merino leather). Both the new options were from the BMW Individual catalogue. A total of seventeen choices therefore remained available.

Colour	Code	Colour	Code
Amarone Merino leather	8025168	Platinum Merino leather	8020297
Black complete Merino leather	X3SW	Polar Gray Merino leather	8025170
Black complete Merino leather (perforated)	X2SW	Portland Brown complete Merino leather	X3BI
Black extended Merino leather	LKSW	Rust Brown Merino leather	8029970
Champagne Merino leather	8025169	Silverstone II complete Merino leather	X3A9
Indianapolis Red complete Merino leather	X3A7	Silverstone II complete Merino leather (perforated)	X2A9
Light Sepang Bronze complete Merino leather	X3A8	Silverstone II extended Merino leather	LKA9
Light Sepang Bronze complete Merino leather (perforated)	X2A8	Syrah Blue Merino leather	8029969
Light Sepang Bronze extended Merino leather (perforated)	LKA8		

Notes:

(1) There were eleven upholstery options that were exclusive to BMW M. The three basic colours were Black, Light Sepang Bronze and Silverstone II, and all three were available with extended, complete and complete (perforated) leather coverage, making nine options. The remaining two colours (Indianapolis Red and Portland Brown) were available only in the 'complete' style.

(2) There were eight BMW Individual upholstery colour options. These were Amarone Merino leather, Caramel Merino leather, Champagne Merino leather, Light Ecru Merino leather, Platinum Merino leather, Polar Gray Merino leather, Rust Brown Merino leather and Syrah Blue Merino leather. All were available with either extended or complete leather coverage (but not in perforated form), making a total of sixteen options. The BMW Individual options were not available in every country where the M5 was sold.

CHAPTER SEVEN

THE F10 TURBOCHARGED CARS

BMW revealed the concept version of its fifth-generation M5 at the Shanghai Auto Show in April 2011, in a clear indication of its anticipation that the Chinese market would become an important one for the new car. It then released advance press information in June, and showed the car at the Nürburgring 24 Hours endurance race towards the end of that month. Various other special viewings, at the Goodwood Festival of Speed and the M Driving Experience at the Salzburgring, were also fitted in over the summer as part of the build-up to the introduction of the production car at the Frankfurt Motor Show in September. North American buyers then saw it at the Los Angeles Motor Show in November.

The build-up to the launch had deliberately been protracted, not least because would-be M5 buyers had once again been made to wait for the new model. The F10 M5 officially went on sale in November 2011, but realistically it was December before the first customers in Europe took delivery. So the best part of two years separated one generation of M5 from the next; the last E60 M5 saloons had been built in December 2009.

This time, there would be only saloons, as no Touring version was slated for production. BMW had been particularly concerned about slow sales of the E61 M5 Touring in the USA, and various company pronouncements had suggested that the F07 GT version of the F10 models might replace estate derivatives altogether in the USA. But there was no chance that this tall, slightly ungainly hatchback model would ever wear an M5 badge.

THE F10 5 SERIES

The F10 was the sixth generation of BMW's 5 Series, and made its debut in November 2009 as a 2010 model. The F10 code was used only for the saloon models, and there were two related derivatives: the F11 Touring estate and the F07 GT hatchback model. There was also a special long-wheelbase saloon for China and Mexico with an extra 140mm (5.5in) of length that provided a cheaper alternative to the 7 Series.

All versions of the new 5 Series depended on BMW's common architecture strategy, adopted to minimize development effort and cost and also to reduce complication in parts logistics and dealer technician training. So the basic platform of the F10 family of 5 Series models was shared with four other BMW models, the F01 7 Series and the F06 (Gran Coupé), F12 (convertible) and F13 (coupé) 6 Series cars. Some of these were introduced after the 5 Series itself. However, at the launch of the F10 models, project engineer Josef Wüst was at some pains to tell journalists that this was not 'platform-sharing' as conventionally understood. Rather was it the use of a backbone technology that permitted technology-sharing among several models. The distinction was a fine one, and probably reflected BMW's worries that customers might think it was using too many common components across its myriad different ranges.

Suspension for all these ranges featured unequal-length aluminium wishbones with ball-joints at the front, and a multi-link rear layout that was a version of BMW's so-called V-axle design. On the 5 Series, the cars were slightly larger than their predecessors, with an extra 80mm (3.15in) of wheelbase, and had an all-steel monocoque body shell. Inevitably, they were therefore somewhat heavier than their predecessors, which had aluminium front-end structures.

Well aware that some of the design ideas favoured by chief designer Chris Bangle had proved controversial, BMW management wanted a more traditional design for the sixth-generation 5 Series. The lead designer under Bangle was Jacek Fröhlich, and work began in November 2005 for a production sign-off in December 2006. Traditional BMW styling cues included creases in the bonnet and below the doors, and the boot was also more conventionally shaped, avoiding the distinctive bustle-back style of the E60 (known rather less than affectionately as the 'Bangle butt' in the USA). On

THE F10 TURBOCHARGED CARS

The F10 models of the 5 Series were introduced for the 2010 Model Year. Styling made deliberate use of traditional BMW cues, but the flat tops to the headlamp units were among the features that earned criticism. BMW

the outside, the car had a strong family resemblance to the E90 3 Series and to the F01 7 Series models, with curvaceous headlamp units and LED tail lamps that presented a distinctive signature from behind.

Inside the cabin, the centre section of the dashboard was angled slightly towards the driver, although less noticeably than in the E28, E34 and E39 5 Series models that had inspired this design feature. Generally, though, the dashboard presented a clean and uncluttered look, with a large colour screen for the ConnectedDrive infotainment system that provided satellite navigation with real-time traffic information, radio selection and internet connection, and acted as a touchscreen alternative to the iDrive rotary control mounted next to the gear selector on the centre console. All models came as standard with front, front-side and full-length side curtain airbags, and other features were active head restraints and a tyre pressure monitoring system. A useful new option was rear seats with a 40/20/40 split folding capability.

As always, the range was built around a long list of both petrol and diesel engines. Several of the petrol engines were turbocharged, and at the top of the petrol range was a 550i model with a turbocharged 4.4-litre V8 engine that delivered 407PS and 600Nm (442lb ft) of torque – figures that put to shame all M5s up to and including the E39s of 1998–2003. Also notable was that the range would introduce the first M-badged diesel models in March 2012, the M550d with 381PS and 740Nm (546lb ft) from a triple-turbo 2993cc straight-six being the most powerful variant.

Across the range, the standard gearboxes were six-speed manuals or eight-speed ZF automatics, and several models were available with the option of the xDrive four-wheel-drive system. All models came with a variety of electronic traction and stability control systems, and with electric

135

■ THE F10 TURBOCHARGED CARS

power-assisted steering incorporating Servotronic. The standard 17-inch wheels carried conventional tyres, but the optional 18-inch and 19-inch styles came with run-flat types. The Efficient Dynamics suite of technologies meanwhile provided an optimum gear-change indicator, active aerodynamics, on-demand ancillaries and brake energy regeneration. Also standard was an electronic parking brake with a self-release function when the car moved off from rest under power.

LOOKING AT THE F10 M5

True to form, the F10 M5 was visually understated – although there was no mistaking it for any other variant of the F10 5 Series. The most obvious difference was at the front, where the three wide air intakes gave the appropriate impression of power, while adaptive Bi-Xenon headlights (recognizable only from close up) were standard wear. Fluted sills below the doors and a discreet boot lid spoiler all contributed to the overall impression that this was a high-performance car, but the most obvious feature from behind was the four exhaust tips, arranged in pairs on either side of the car and poking out from the deeper-than-standard rear valance under neat flares in the panel. Interestingly, this was the first M5 to be made available with a tow-bar option, something that BMW M had stoutly resisted since 1984.

The standard wheels were 19-inch multi-spoke alloys, 2 inches larger in diameter than the standard F10 offerings. However, unlike the optional 19-inch wheels on mainstream 5 Series, these wheels came with conventional Michelin Super Sport tyres and not run-flat types. As was by now expected on an M5, those at the rear had wider rims and tyres than those at the front. There was also a 20-inch wheel option, with a split five-spoke design. Neither size was accompanied by a spare tyre; instead, each M5 was

A redesigned front apron with large air intakes, and those gills in the front wings made the M5 derivative of the E60 immediately recognizable. BMW

THE F10 TURBOCHARGED CARS

The side gills were also used to house turn signals and an M5 logo. BMW

The deep intakes in the front air dam were unique to M5 versions of the F10 5 Series. BMW

The M5 came with 19-inch multi-spoke alloy wheels as standard, running on Michelin Pilot Super Sport tyres. As always, there was an M logo incorporated in the design of the wheel. The ventilated and cross-drilled front brake disc is visible here, and so is the blue-enamelled brake caliper. BMW

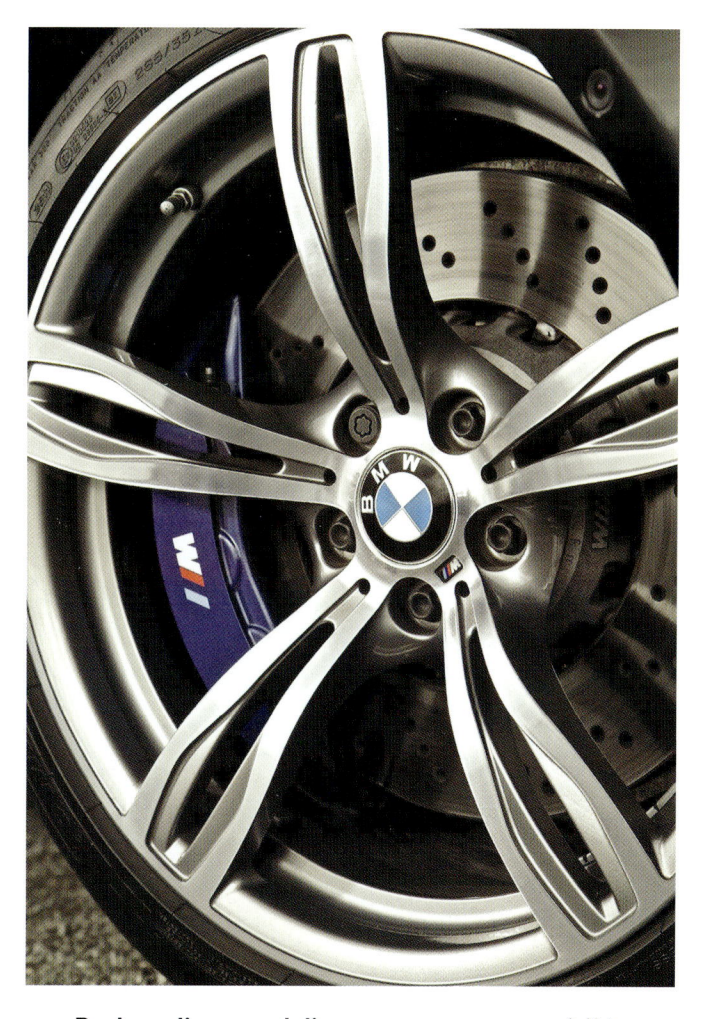

Brake calipers and discs were even more visible through the paired spokes of the 20-inch wheels. BMW

THE F10 TURBOCHARGED CARS

provided with a mobility kit in the boot. If that was unable to deal with a puncture (as would occur, for example, if the tyre was badly damaged), the M5 driver had to call for roadside assistance.

What onlookers could not see, of course, were the changes under the M5's skin. These included a special front cross-member, stiffened and attached by two additional bolts. The differential mounting was also unique to the car, and was fixed rigidly to the body shell in order to eliminate the movement inherent in the standard F10's rubber bush mountings. All these changes made the wheelbase of the M5 11mm shorter than that of the mainstream F10 saloons.

The four tailpipes peeping out from the rear apron were the most obvious recognition feature from behind, especially if the M5 badge had been deleted. BMW

THE F10 TURBOCHARGED CARS

The underside was also braced by unique stiffening rods and shear plates, and weight was saved as far as possible by forging the new components from aluminium alloy. Even so, the new car was noticeably heavier than the model it replaced, and received some criticism for it.

Then, of course, the new M5 had its own special engine and transmission.

THE S63 V8 TWIN POWER TURBO ENGINE

Increasingly strict international emissions requirements were the main reason why BMW chose not to develop the S85 V10 engine any further for the F10 version of the M5. Instead, they did the almost unthinkable, and developed a smaller-capacity V8 engine to which they added twin turbochargers, so making the 2012-model M5 the first of its kind to be turbocharged. BMW claimed that emissions were cut by 25 per cent over those of the outgoing V10 engine.

If the switch to turbocharging surprised many enthusiasts of the M brand, it need not have done. In fact, the twin-turbocharged V8 had already been seen in the X5M and X6M models from BMW, and was already being called the Twin Power Turbo engine. It was, though, something of a surprise that the M5 was not the car in which the engine made its debut; marketing priorities, particularly in the USA where the SUV models sold strongly, had seen to that. Nevertheless, M5 enthusiasts were treated to something special, because the Twin Power Turbo had been further uprated for its F10 application. The result was the most powerful road car that the M division had ever produced.

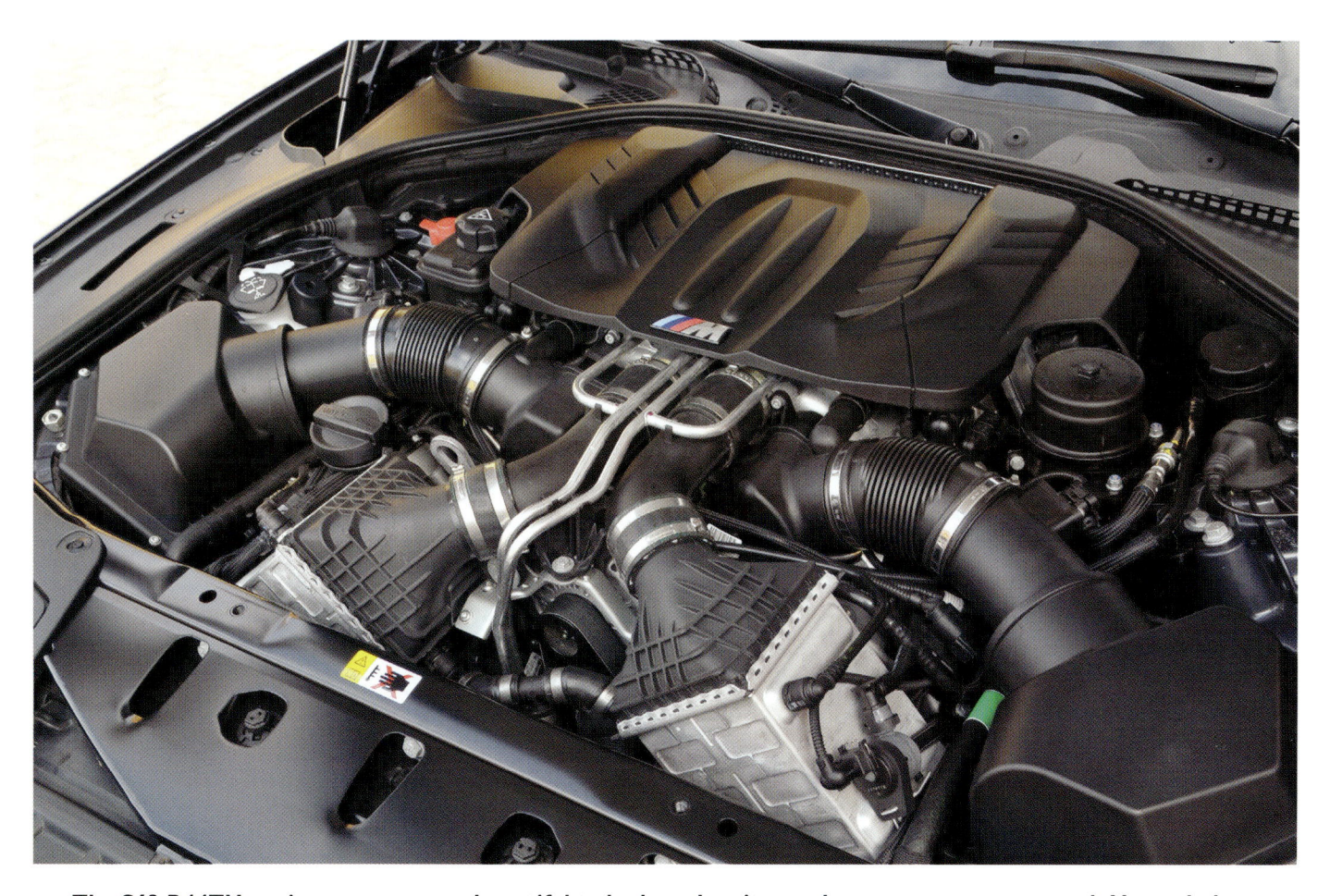

The S63 B44TU engine was no more beautiful to look at than its cumbersome name suggested. Nevertheless, the M division had done their best. Those 'boxes' at the front of the engine bay were the intercoolers for the twin turbochargers and, as usual, much of the hardware was concealed underneath a plastic cover. BMW

139

THE F10 TURBOCHARGED CARS

The basis of the new engine was BMW's N63 4395cc V8, originally introduced in 2008 and now extensively modified by the M division to incorporate those twin turbochargers. The early versions of the S63 B44 in the X5M and X6M models made clear that even BMW M was now going to rely on turbocharging to gain extra power – a strategy really dictated by pressure on motor manufacturers to reduce fuel consumption. Where the mainstream N63 engine in the 550i depended on a single turbocharger, however, the S63 engine used twin turbochargers. Both were twin-scroll types, made by Honeywell and mounted in the vee between the cylinder banks to create an engine as compact as possible. Both had an air-to-water intercooler rather than the more common air-to-air type, because these were more efficient and in this installation gave a shorter distance for the cooled air to travel. A pulse-tuned exhaust manifold was carefully arranged to give a constant flow of gas across the turbochargers.

For the M5, the S63 B44 engine gained direct fuel injection, a higher compression ratio, stronger pistons, a higher turbo boost of 22psi, and Valvetronic, the BMW variable-lift valve system that was introduced on mainstream 5 Series models as well (see sidebar). Lack of space under the bonnet meant that the engine management computer used on the X5M and X6M models had to be split into two units, and these Bosch-manufactured ECUs were mounted on the engine next to the catalytic converters where water cooling maintained acceptable temperatures. All these changes turned the engine into an S63 B44TU type, and the headline figures were 560PS between 6,000 and 7,000rpm, with 680Nm (502lb ft) of torque between 1,500 and 5,750rpm.

Yet despite these huge power and torque outputs, there was one disappointing feature of the engine. The twin turbochargers had the effect of muting its exhaust noise to the point where it sounded like a four-cylinder at speed. Even tuning work on the exhaust system failed to produce the right sound for an M5, and the M division was forced to resort to subterfuge. The twin-turbo M5s all came with what BMW called Active Sound – which played more appropriate engine noises through the speakers of the car's ICE system! The volume and frequency of this artificial engine noise was determined by parameters including engine speed, throttle load and road speed, all of them taken directly from the engine management ECUs. Needless to say, not all M5 enthusiasts were keen on this idea.

Nevertheless, some features did meet universal approval, and one was the use of a decent-sized (80-litre) fuel tank. In tandem with the new engine's much-improved fuel economy (BMW claimed it was 30 per cent less thirsty than the V10), this gave the new M5 a realistic range of around 300 miles, and was a vast improvement on the undersized tank in the E60 and E61 cars. Another welcome change was that the 250km/h speed limiter that was standard wear could be over-ridden by the optional M Driver's Package, which restricted the car to 305km/h (190mph) – still, in fact, short of the 330km/h (205mph) that a fully derestricted car could supposedly achieve. BMW themselves reported that the new F10 car could lap the Nürburgring race track, where much of the development work had been done, in seven minutes and fifty-five seconds – eighteen seconds faster than its V10-engined E60 predecessor.

VALVETRONIC

BMW's Valvetronic system is a variable valve timing system that gives continuous control over the amount of lift of the individual intake valves on each cylinder. BMW claim that the system precisely regulates the quantity of air entering the cylinders for optimum performance, and also eliminates the pumping losses and airflow disturbance caused by a conventional throttle butterfly. Valvetronic improves cold start behaviour, lowers exhaust emissions and provides smoother, more immediate power. By optimizing the fuel/air mix process, it can also deliver fuel savings of up to 10 per cent.

Valvetronic uses a stepper motor to control a secondary eccentric shaft fitted with a series of intermediate rocker arms, which in turn control the degree of valve lift. This secondary eccentric shaft, sometimes described as an extra camshaft, is electronically actuated. The throttle butterfly is no longer needed as a means of controlling the air supply, although for safety reasons it is still fitted as an emergency back-up.

On the S63 B44TU engine, Valvetronic is used in addition to the Double-VANOS variable camshaft system.

THE F10 TURBOCHARGED CARS

THE M-DCT TRANSMISSION

By the time the F10 M5 was under development, BMW had decided that it could go no further with the SMG gearbox that had been used in the E60 and E61 M5s and in contemporary versions of the M3. So it worked with gearbox specialist Getrag to develop a new two-pedal transmission that would give faster shifts than the human hand could achieve and would also give the option of manual control through Formula 1-style paddles on the steering wheel.

What came out of the collaboration was a dual-clutch transmission with electronic control, and it was first introduced as an option on the E90 M3 models in April 2008, more than three years before it became available on an M5. In fact, even that was not the first appearance of a dual-clutch transmission, as the first ones had been brought to market in 2003 by Volkswagen, who had worked with Borg Warner to develop a system for their Golf model. Dual-clutch systems worked by using concentric clutches, which acted on alternate gears in the transmission; their main advance was that they allowed lightning-fast gear-changes with no interruption of the torque flow from the engine. With an electronic control system, the dual-clutch transmission could be used as a fully automatic gearbox while giving manual override control to a degree that was simply not possible in conventional automatics with a torque converter.

Contemporary BMW manual gearboxes had six forward speeds, but the E60 and E61 M5s had seven-speed SMG gearboxes, and no smaller number of gears would do for the replacement model. So the BMW dual-clutch transmission was also developed with seven speeds. Manufacture was handled by Getrag, and the new gearbox incorporated a Borg Warner DualTronic twin-clutch module. It came with the name of M-DKG in Germany; the letters stood for

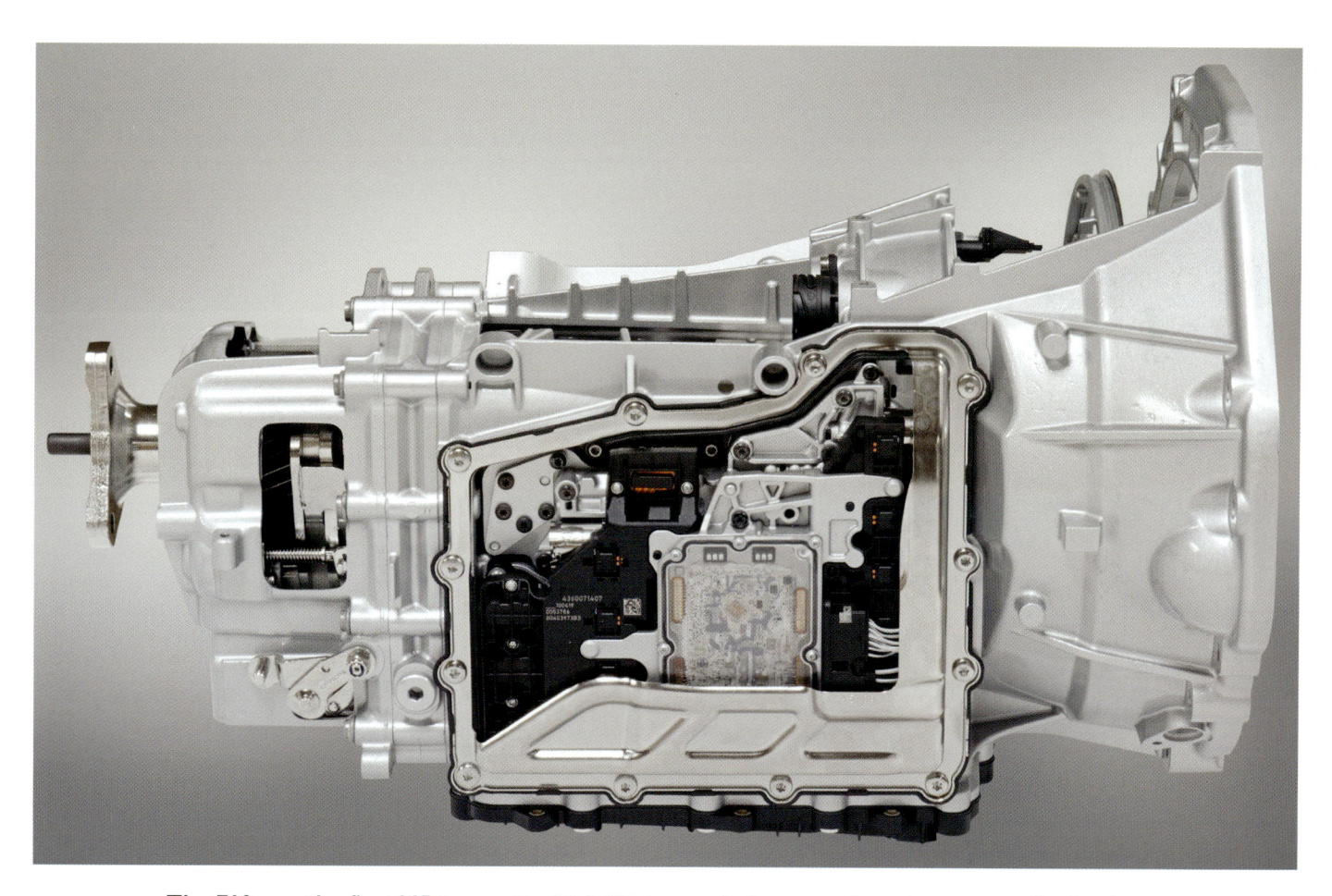

The F10 was the first M5 to use the M-DCT transmission, seen here in cutaway display form. Note the size of the circuit board displayed in the sectioned area nearest the camera! BMW

141

THE F10 TURBOCHARGED CARS

M Doppel-Kupplungs-Getriebe, which stood quite literally for M Double-Clutch Transmission, and that was the name given to it in English. In the English-speaking countries it was generally known as the M-DCT type, or more commonly simply as the DCT.

The earlier SMG gearboxes had been accompanied by Drivelogic, and the system was added to the new DCT transmission as well. Drivelogic on the F10 M5 offered three settings, which could delay upshifts and alter other parameters to give a more sporting feel.

Right from the start, however, the M division anticipated that US buyers might not take to the new DCT transmission. As Chapter 6 explains, customer pressure had led to BMW making a manual gearbox available on E60 M5s for North America, and this time the M division did not wait to be asked. They made a six-speed gearbox available on the F10 M5 as an option from the beginning – but only in North America. There is more about it later in this chapter.

DRIVING DYNAMICS

An especially interesting feature of the M5 was that it dispensed with many of the active chassis systems that made the mainstream F10 models so good to drive. In place of the mainstream cars' variable-ratio electro-mechanical power steering, the M5 had electro-hydraulic power steering. Instead of passive rear-wheel steering and active anti-roll bars, it had an essentially simple version of the double-wishbone, multi-link layout. The front track was wider than standard, there were progressive rate springs and adaptive dampers, and the caster and camber settings were specially calibrated to give extra sharpness to the steering. However, the M5 did come with the M division's own Active M Differential, a variable-lock torque-vectoring differential that replaced the more conventional locking differentials seen on earlier M cars.

Those big 19-inch wheels covered brakes that were larger than the mainstream F10 issue, of course. Ventilated all round, and cross-drilled as well on the front, all of them were of the two-piece 'floating' design used on earlier M5s. For maximum braking effect, each of the monobloc front calipers had six asymmetrically sized pistons, and for maximum visual effect each one was also painted blue. From the start, larger-diameter carbon-ceramic brake discs were available as an optional extra. At a cost of well over £7,000 in the UK, they demanded financial commitment as well as enthusiasm.

This cutaway shows the elements of the Active M Differential that was standard on the F10 M5. Note, too, the special aluminium mounting cradle. BMW

THE F10 TURBOCHARGED CARS

The facia of this UK right-hand-drive model shows how the centre of the dash was angled slightly towards the driver. The multi-function screen was neatly integrated into the design, as on other F10s. The iDrive control and gear selector swapped sides on left-hand-drive models. BMW

The new M5 came with the expected suite of electronic systems that could vary the car's responses to suit the driver. So M Dynamic Mode could be used to vary the intervention of the stability control system, raising its threshold to allow more wheelspin and tail-out cornering; it could also switch the system off altogether. Dynamic Damper Control offered three settings – Comfort, Sport and Sport Plus – for the electronic damper control system, and M Servotronic likewise offered three settings for the steering. These were Comfort, Sport and Sport Plus, and they varied the amount of effort necessary at the wheel. There were also three accelerator settings, labelled Efficient, Sport and Sport Plus, which altered the accelerator response. Their effect was accompanied by changes in the engine-noise soundtrack played through the speakers of the Active Sound system.

ON THE INSIDE

As always, the basic cabin architecture of the M5 was the same as in lesser 5 Series models, and there were M5-branded kick-plates on the door sills to remind anybody entering the car that this was no ordinary F10 model. However, on this occasion BMW could not be accused of overemphasizing the special nature of the M5 on the inside, and on the instrument panel only the rev counter carried the M logo.

Nevertheless, the centre console had a unique layout to accommodate the shift stick and associated button controls of the DCT transmission. A rotary control on the passenger's side gave access to the functions displayed on the large screen in the centre of the dashboard, and of course this control swapped sides depending on whether the car was built with left-hand or right-hand drive.

■ THE F10 TURBOCHARGED CARS

Sill plates with the M5 logo reminded passengers that this was the high-performance version of the latest 5 Series car. BMW

Practical as ever, the F10 M5 came with a capacious boot. BMW

The rear seats offered plenty of legroom and a luxurious ambience as well. The centre armrest opened up to reveal a storage compartment and the obligatory cupholders. BMW

144

THE F10 TURBOCHARGED CARS

The speedometer read to 330km/h, although the car was limited to 250km/h as standard, and there was an M logo on the rev counter. The legends for the read-outs below the dials came in different languages for different markets; this is a German-market car. BMW

ABOVE: **This close-up shows the selector lever for the M-DCT gearbox, the control for the electronic parking brake, and the rotary control for the iDrive system.** BMW

CENTRE: **BMW's iDrive had been heavily criticized when it first appeared as being too complicated and much less intuitive to use than its makers claimed. By the time of the F10, additional selector buttons were used to supplement the rotary control.** BMW

ABOVE: **The keyless start system required the driver to have the transponder fob in a pocket, or anywhere else in the car. This button then started and stopped the engine.** BMW

145

The standard front seats were wide sports types with multi-way adjustment, and the interior came as standard with soft Merino leather in 'extended' configuration. There was, as always, a choice of trim materials that included brushed aluminium and wood options. All part of the M5's standard equipment were a DAB radio, the BMW Professional satellite navigation system and a head-up display that showed vital driver information in an easily visible area of the windscreen. In addition, Surround View cameras (actually located near the front wheels) could be used to give a view down the flanks of the car when this would help slow-speed manoeuvring.

PRODUCTION CHANGES

At the time of writing in early 2015, the F10 M5 had been on sale for rather less than three years, and there had been just one minor facelift in autumn 2013. Worth noting, though, is that BMW briefly halted sales of the 2013-model cars in late September 2012 while it rectified a production problem. Only vehicles built between 19 July and 11 September that year were affected, and all those already sold to customers were recalled to have the problem dealt with under warranty. The problem was caused by an incorrect tolerance in the oil pump that could cause the pump's driveshaft to separate from its rotor, leading to a sudden and potentially catastrophic loss of oil pressure.

The autumn 2013 facelift brought a redesigned grille, new paint colours, new leather options and new interior trims. An additional option was adaptive LED headlights. The biggest change was the arrival of an optional Competition Package, which had really been introduced to fight off increasing competition from rival high-performance saloons such as the latest Jaguar XF-R S and the Mercedes-Benz E63 AMG S. The Competition Package brought more engine power, lowered and stiffened suspension, and some cosmetic changes as well.

The S63 engine in Competition Package guise now delivered 580PS as compared to the 560PS of the standard tune, although the maximum torque of 680Nm remained unchanged. The M division had clearly been working on the F10 M5's disappointing exhaust note, too, because the exhaust system had been changed to deliver a more exciting sound – though not enough for the piped engine noises to become unnecessary. The ride height was lowered by 10mm (0.4in), and the springs, dampers and anti-roll bars were all uprated. The 20-inch alloy wheels were standard wear, and the M Dynamic mode was recalibrated, giving bespoke MDM, ESC and Active M Differential settings and hydraulic power-steering mapping. For good measure, black exhaust tips were added as well, and BMW claimed that the 0–100km/h (0–62mph) acceleration time was cut to 4.2 seconds. *Car* magazine in South Africa actually achieved better than that when it tested one for its May 2014 issue, recording a time of 4.1 seconds.

However, *Autocar* (8 April 2014) in the UK was not impressed by the fact that the Competition Package in this £80,205 car did not include 'the one thing this car desperately needs if you're going to fully deploy its power and weight on a circuit: better brakes. Standard M5 brakes have long been about as useful on track as chocolate crockery.' So that was why those carbon-ceramic brakes had been made available as an option.

THE RHD CARS

Right-hand-drive versions of the F10 M5 reached showrooms in the UK in November 2011 with a base price of £73,040. In Australia, the car was launched to the press in February 2012 at the Phillip Island Grand Prix track.

All the right-hand-drive F10 M5s were built with the same FV92 specification. No sales figures were available at the time of writing.

THE NORTH AMERICAN CARS

Even though it was the largest potential market for the new M5, North America had to wait. Production of the North American variants did not begin until March 2012, nearly six months after that of the European versions, and the car went on sale in the USA and in Canada in early September that year as a 2013 model. The base price was $90,695.

Side marker lights aside, the North American F10 M5 was essentially the same car as the European version. However, as noted earlier, it was made available with a six-speed manual gearbox as a no-cost alternative to the seven-speed DCT transmission. In the early years, this accounted for about one in every ten M5 orders, a statistic that rather suggests that North American buyers were not as averse to the DCT transmission as BMW had feared they might be. In any case, the company did make known that this was the last time such a gearbox would be offered.

THE F10 TURBOCHARGED CARS

modes, the engine management system blipped the throttle on downshifts to match the speed to the new gear, but in Sport Plus mode it did not. A later assessment by the same magazine in February 2014 reported that the manual gearbox 'makes you feel more involved in getting the best out of [the car]'.

SPECIAL EDITIONS

The M Performance Edition (2012)

The M Performance Edition was a special limited edition for the UK only, and was announced on 31 May 2012 in tandem with an M Performance Edition of the M3 coupé. Despite the name, neither of these cars added improved performance to the basic package. Instead, both showcased some of the options available from BMW Individual, the marketing idea being that buyers who could not quite stretch to the base price of the special edition (over £95,000 for the M5) might at least choose some of its special options for a less expensive standard-production model.

There were just thirty of these cars, available in the same red, white or blue colours as the M3 M Performance Edition. The colours themselves were all matt 'Frozen' types from the BMW Individual range, and there were ten cars in Japan Red with a Frozen Red wrap, ten in Frozen White and ten in Frozen Blue. These colours were set off by Dark Chrome grille surrounds, side gills and exhaust tips, by Matt Black alloy wheels with the 20-inch M Double-Spoke design, and by dark sun-protection glass.

All three colours came with full Merino leather upholstery in Black, with contrasting Mugello Red, Lotus White or Tobago Blue stitching to match the exterior paint. Interior trim was in Piano Black from the BMW individual range, with a laser-cut 'One of 30' legend; as a matter of policy, BMW had decided not to number special-edition cars individually any more. The front seats were M Sport multi-function types with lumbar support, and the rear seat had the split-fold option. The door sills made clear that this was a 'BMW M Performance Edition', and the front head restraints had M stitching. Additional details, so much appreciated by the buyers of BMW M cars, were floor mats with contrast piping and Alcantara trim on the rim of the steering wheel. The cars came with internet connection, the BMW Professional twelve-speaker ICE system, USB audio telephone interface, mobile application preparation and a speed-limit display.

Positively the last time they would provide a manual gearbox on an M5 – or so BMW said when they made the six-speed available for North America. BMW

The six-speed gearbox was an uprated version of the one available in the 550i model, and it took about 15kg (33lb) of weight out of the car, also moving the weight bias very slightly towards the rear. According to BMW M President Dr Friedrich Nitschke, there was also some special software in the installation that electronically protected the gearbox if the driver missed a gear-change.

When *BMW Car* magazine tried a manual-gearbox M5 for its March 2013 issue, it reported that the car was fractionally slower than the DCT type, reaching 60mph from rest in 4.3 seconds without using the Launch Control. The clutch was surprisingly light, but the manual gearbox also helped to reveal a hint of turbocharger lag below 3,000rpm that the DCT transmission normally masked. In Normal and Sport

THE F10 TURBOCHARGED CARS

WHAT THE PRESS THOUGHT

Autocar, 8 April 2014

'It's capable of remarkably well-mannered refinement and ease of use one moment, and then absolutely first-order grip, iron body control and incredible performance the next.'

'"Comfort" mode engages on the Drive Performance Control module as a default when you start the engine and move off … Move upwards into "Sport" and "Sport+" modes on the steering, powertrain, chassis and DSC systems and purposefulness quickly muscles its way into the driving experience. Most notably, the [steering] wheel goes from heavy to absurdly heavy if you let it, and the ride quality loses that pleasing compliance entirely, riveting the M5's body to the ground on smooth surfaces, but making it crash and jolt unhelpfully on anything less-than-smooth.'

'[A highlight is] the sense of incredible outright speed the car delivers at full power. Partly because the engine's so docile under less throttle, but mostly because there's just so much grunt, the M5 never fails to amaze when you downshift a couple of times and bury the pedal … Magnificent, really.'

Autocar, online

'The seven-speed, dual-clutch M DCT transmission … endows the car with relaxed usability to match its superb at-pace precision. It will remain in auto mode whichever of the powertrain presets you choose, but nudge one of the standard wheel-mounted paddles and it will shift to manual, in which state it will hold its gears as expected and swap ratios on command with impressive response and precision.

'Also, there's a low-speed assistance mode via which you can make the M5 creep at ideal manoeuvring speed with a quick stab of the accelerator. This will make this M5 significantly easier to live with (read, park) than the last.'

'The BMW's standard fit brakes … are prone to fade after a tough workout. The solution is on the options list, in the shape of a set of carbon-ceramic brakes. The setup is ferociously costly, but they couple decent pedal feel with reliable stopping power.'

'You'll get better than 28mpg from the car at a conservative cruise – vastly better than the 22mpg of the old BMW M5 – and an 80-litre fuel tank means a real-world range is now on the right side of 300 miles to a full tank.'

Evo, October 2011

'The motor [emits] the strangest combination of sounds I think I have ever heard in a car. That almost-V10 tune gives way to a plain, vulgar drone on small throttle openings at town speeds – you'd swear it only had four cylinders.'

'This M DCT Drivelogic wot-not is an exceptional transmission – the best ever fitted to a fast saloon car.'

'Just as the torque curve subsides, so the power takes over and the result must be one of the most remarkable powertrains of modern times … the advantages it offers in the mid-range, being turbocharged, are entirely appropriate for this car.'

'This car feels notably heavier than its predecessor, despite some serious modifications over the standard 5 Series.'

'A question mark hangs over the car's balance of ride comfort and roll stiffness, but not enough to dampen the overwhelming feeling of wellbeing you get when you drive it for several hours.'

Car and Driver, November 2011

(The car tested was a European-specification model, and the magazine achieved a 3.7-second 0–60mph time by using the Launch Control system.)

'Launch Control automatically dumps the clutch at about 3,000 rpm and upshifts for you. When we finally did it right, the quarter-mile went down in 12 seconds flat at 122 mph. In another 6.3 seconds, the car was passing 150 mph.'

'You cannot select a gear, push a pedal, or turn the wheel in the new M5 without assistance from the many watchful computers monitoring your every bodily twitch … [but] … BMW goes to lengths to make the electronic boundary layer between you and the machine transparent, or, at least, subject to an off button. And if you forget that nearly everything you're feeling, hearing, and doing has been run through a microprocessor, the car … is a nice place to be.'

'Stand down the stability control entirely and watch the M5 bonfire its tires drifting sideways, spitting smoke and chunks of expensive Michelin Pilot Super Sport rubber.'

'The previous V-10 had an 8,250-rpm redline. With the M Twin Power Turbo, Elvis pretty much leaves the building at 6000, though the revs go to 7,200rpm, supposedly for track-day lappers who like to hold gears longer – and, we suspect, to uphold the M tradition of making spin-dizzy engines.'

Road & Track, April 2014

(The car tested had the Competition Package.)

'The M5 is beautiful, its stance muscular, proportions perfect … and its interior isn't just gorgeous, it boasts iDrive, our favorite infotainment interface in the business.'

'Thanks to the world's most difficult-to-activate launch control, plus the double whammy of turbo torque and two-wheel drive, the BMW is a torment on the drag strip … But the M5 does the deed [0–60mph] in just 3.8 seconds.'

'The M5's suspension is oversprung and underdamped, and without question, the engine makes more power than the chassis can handle … The M5 is blazingly fast and yet miserable to launch.'

Car South Africa, May 2014

'The CP [Competition Package] exhaust enhances the low-speed burble and percussive pops accompanying gearshifts when accelerating in anger.'

'With astounding reserves of power and torque on tap, the CP-endowed BMW needs a skilled driver at the helm to delve into its dynamic abilities, especially when disabling the stability control.'

'The seven-speed, dual-clutch transmission is state of the art and its characteristics can be altered between seamless shifts to race car-like whiplashes depending on the chosen setting.'

■ THE F10 TURBOCHARGED CARS

BMW showcased its 'Frozen' paint finishes on the M Performance Edition. This was one of the ten blue cars for the UK. BMW GB

The M Performance Edition for the UK also included white cars. The contrasting dark colours of the exhaust tips and the rear diffuser are seen to good effect here. BMW GB

All the M Performance Edition cars came with special sill plates and a special interior reminder that this was 'One of 30' cars; it was no longer BMW policy to number limited edition cars individually. BMW GB

Other standard features on these limited-edition cars included keyless Comfort Access and soft-close doors, powered boot-lid operation, a reversing camera and High Beam Assistant (automatic headlamp dipping). BMW UK publicity claimed that the M Performance Edition came with £22,075 worth of otherwise-optional equipment as standard – a figure that would have comfortably paid for a brand-new BMW 1 Series car at the time – and that the car combined 'track-car dynamics with supreme touring comfort'.

The Nighthawk Edition (2013)

The Nighthawk Edition was a very special limited edition of ten cars for Japan, announced in October 2013. All cars had Frozen Black paint from the BMW Individual catalogue, with a Dark Chrome finish for the grilles, side gills and door handles. LED headlights were standard. The interior was upholstered in Sakhir Orange full Merino leather, and came with M Performance carbon trim on the doors and the instrument panel. A serial number badge was also part of the package.

The mechanical specification included the Competition Package, but without the special wheels that normally came with it. The 580PS engine drove through the standard seven-speed M-DCT gearbox, and the carbon-ceramic brake option was fitted as standard. The Nighthawk cars all came with BMW's Driver Assistance Package, and the base price in Japan was 18,200,000 Yen.

The 30 Jahre Edition (2014)

BMW decided to celebrate the thirtieth anniversary of the very first M5 with the release of a worldwide special edition in May 2014. There were to be 300 of these cars, known as the 30 Jahre Edition (30 Years Edition) and they were equipped with both performance and cosmetic details that made them unique among the F10 M5s. The UK received thirty examples, each one priced at £91,890 before any of the optional extras were added.

■ THE F10 TURBOCHARGED CARS

ABOVE: **The 30 Jahre Edition makes clear how the paint finish can alter the appearance of a car. Contrast the Frozen Dark Silver here with the bright blue seen on page 136.** BMW

LEFT: **The 30 Jahre Edition came with two-tone alloy wheels and with special gold-finished brake calipers bearing the M division's logo.** BMW

THE F10 TURBOCHARGED CARS

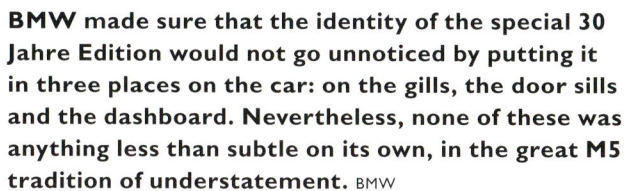

BMW made sure that the identity of the special 30 Jahre Edition would not go unnoticed by putting it in three places on the car: on the gills, the door sills and the dashboard. Nevertheless, none of these was anything less than subtle on its own, in the great M5 tradition of understatement. BMW

BELOW: Unmistakably F10 M5, but also unmistakably the 30 Jahre Edition ... Compare this with the picture on page 143 to see how subtle colour and trim changes could make a big difference to the way the dashboard and passenger cabin looked on these cars. BMW

153

■ THE F10 TURBOCHARGED CARS

The cosmetic details mainly came from BMW Individual. All 300 cars had Frozen Dark Silver metallic paint, with contrasting Dark Chrome grille surrounds, side gills, door handle inserts and tailpipes. There were also unique bicolour 20-inch wheels, with the M Double-Spoke design that carried type code 601M. The side gills were further individualized with '30 Jahre M5' badges. From the equipment options list came adaptive LED headlights.

The passenger cabin was characterized by sill plates with the '30 Jahre M5' legend, and of course Comfort Access and smart opener were standard. The upholstery was Black full Merino leather with Black Alcantara, and there was Anthracite Alcantara on the steering wheel, centre console, arm rests and door pulls. The headlining, too, was in Anthracite Alcantara, and the upper and lower sections of the instrument panel were trimmed in Nappa leather. There were M Sport multi-function front seats with lumbar support, and additional 12-volt power sockets in the rear accompanied the split-folding rear seat. All four seat backrests carried the '30 Jahre M5' legend, this time in stitching, while the trim panels were in Dark Aluminum Trace with Dark Chrome finisher. Each car also carried an identification plaque ahead of the front passenger, noting that it was one of 300 examples, and each one came with a Harmon/Kardon sixteen-speaker surround sound system. Customers could choose between a Harmon/Kardon head unit with an output of 600 watts and a 1200-watt Bang & Olufsen system. All cars came with Driving Assistant, and many of the options available for the standard production M5 could also be ordered.

Much more important to hardcore M enthusiasts was that the 30 Jahre Edition came with the most powerful road engine yet produced by the M division. In percentage terms, the improvements were not massive – just over 7 per cent more power to give 600PS and just under 3 per cent more torque to give 700Nm – but at this level of output the gains of 40PS and 20Nm were quite significant. They made this version of the F10 M5 the fastest-ever production model from BMW, with a 0–100km/h (0–62mph) time of 3.9 seconds. Those 600PS were also more than twice the power output of the original E28 M5, which in 1985 had 286PS.

Not surprisingly, the 30 Jahre Edition came with the Competition Package (less its special wheels and 580PS engine tune) as standard. Among the options was – at long last – a further developed exhaust system that was only available for the 30 Jahre Edition. Developed jointly by BMW and Akrapovic, it was a lightweight system made entirely from titanium, and delivered a richer and more powerful sound than the standard exhaust. It normally came with 92mm (3.62in) tailpipes made from polished titanium and bearing the M logo, but for extra cost could be had with 95mm (3.74in) finishers in carbon fibre. The costs were simply eye-watering: the special system cost £6,645 in the UK, rising to £6,890 with the carbon-fibre finishers.

PERFORMANCE FIGURES FOR F10 M5 MODELS

European models	0–100km/h	4.3 sec
	0–60mph	3.7 sec
	Maximum	250km/h (155mph), electronically limited; 305km/h (190mph) with M Driver's Package
With Competition Package	0–100km/h	4.2 sec
30 Jahre Edition	0–100km/h	3.9 sec

In the USA, where the Launch Control was inhibited to a degree, *Motor Trend* magazine found that an M5 saloon could hit 60mph from rest in 4.5 seconds. The figure used by BMW M development chief Albert Biermann in 2010 to Greg Kable of *Autocar* was 4.1 seconds for the 0–100km/h (0–62mph) time.

F10 M5 SPECIFICATIONS

Models
FV91	November 2011 on	LHD European spec
FV92	November 2011 on	RHD European spec
FV93	March 2012 on	LHD North American spec

Engine:
Type S63B44 V8-cylinder petrol
4395cc (89mm x 88.3mm)
Four overhead camshafts; Double-VANOS variable camshaft timing and Valvetronic variable valve lift
Four valves per cylinder
Five-bearing crankshaft
Compression ratio 10.0:1
Twin turbochargers
Bosch engine management system
Exhaust with dual catalytic converters
560PS (552bhp) from 5,750 to 7,000rpm
580PS with Competition Package
600PS for 30 Jahre Edition
680Nm (501lb ft) from 1,500 to 5,750rpm
700Nm for 30 Jahre Edition

Transmission:
Seven-speed M-DCT gearbox
   Ratios 4.81:1, 2.59:1, 1.70:1, 1.28:1, 1.00:1, 0.84:1, 0.67:1
Six-speed ZF Type G manual gearbox available on North American models
   Ratios 4.05:1, 2.40:1, 1.58:1, 1.19:1, 1.00:1, 0.87:1

Axle ratio:
3.15:1 (all types)
(Active M Differential locking system standard on all models)

Suspension, steering and brakes:
Front suspension with double wishbones, MacPherson struts, electronic dampers and anti-roll bar
Multi-link rear suspension with coil springs, electronic dampers and anti-roll bar
Rack-and-pinion steering with lock-dependent ratio (mean ratio 12.4:1) and standard ZF Servotronic speed-variable power assistance
Disc brakes all round, 400mm (15.7in) ventilated on front wheels and 396mm (15.6in) ventilated on rear wheels; 'floating' two-piece discs on all four wheels; six-piston calipers on all wheels; twin hydraulic circuits; ABS standard. Optional 410mm diameter carbon-ceramic brake discs

Dimensions:
Overall length:	4,910mm (193.3in)		Overall height:	1,451mm (57.1in) – saloon
Overall width:	1,891mm (74.4in)		Wheelbase:	2,964mm (116.7in) – saloon

Wheels and tyres:
9J x 19 five-stud alloy front wheels with 265/40ZR19 tyres
10J x 19 five-stud alloy rear wheels with 295/35ZR19 tyres
Optional 20-inch wheels with 265/35ZR20 (front) and 295/30ZR20 (rear)

Kerb weights:
Saloon   1,870kg (4,122lb)

■ THE F10 TURBOCHARGED CARS

PAINT AND INTERIOR OPTIONS

Names are shown in their English forms throughout.

Paints from November 2011

There were eight standard paint colours available at launch.

Colour	Code	Colour	Code
Alpine White III	300	Monte Carlo Blue metallic	B05
Black Sapphire metallic	475	Silverstone II metallic	A29
Havana metallic	A17	Singapore Gray metallic	B41
Imperial Blue metallic	A89	Space Gray metallic	A52

A further range of eight colours could be ordered from the BMW Individual catalogue.

Colour	Code	Colour	Code
Amazonite Silver metallic	X07	Citrine Black metallic	X02
Azurite Black metallic	S34	Frozen Gray metallic	U83
Brilliant White metallic	U21	Frozen Silver metallic	490/W07
Champagne Quartz metallic	X08	Moonstone metallic	X04

Interior colours from November 2011

There were six standard options at launch, with Extended Merino leather and Full Merino leather versions of three colours: Black, Sakhir Orange and Silverstone.

In addition, there were five colours of Merino leather available from the BMW Individual range: Champagne, Cohiba Brown, Graphite, Platinum and Silk Gray.

Headlinings were Black as standard, but there were also four Alcantara options from the BMW Individual range: Anthracite, Champagne, Platinum and Silk Gray.

CHAPTER EIGHT

SO YOU THINK YOU WANT AN M5?

The BMW M5 in all its forms has been one of the most desirable road cars of all for more than thirty years. It combines all the performance and handling of contemporary supercars with the everyday usability of a family saloon, and that combination is a powerful attraction.

However, before setting out on a determined search for an M5 of any vintage, it is important to calm down a moment and to put the car into its context. That car was a very expensive piece of machinery when it was new, aimed at wealthy owners. Those wealthy owners could not only afford to buy the car, but they could afford to run it, which meant covering the high cost of fuel, insurance and maintenance.

Once M5s reached the used-car market, they typically went one of two ways. A few cars went to enthusiasts who were prepared to cope with the high cost of running them

Small details have always added to the delight of the M5 models. This is the tricolour flash on the driver's seat of an E28 model. NICK DIMBLEBY

Well, which one would you want to own? The first four generations of M5 saloon are lined up here for inspection. Every one of them can be bought for very much less than the cost of a new M5, and every one offers the driver a very special ownership experience. BMW

157

SO YOU THINK YOU WANT AN M5?

and maintaining them in tip-top condition. Unfortunately, not every M5 went to such an owner. A good number went to owners who could afford to buy the car, were just about able to manage the fuel and insurance costs, but skimped on the maintenance in order to make ends meet.

As subsequent unfortunate owners have discovered all too often, M5s are high-maintenance cars and demand regular (and often very expensive) attention. If they do not get that attention, the problems gradually mount up until they are completely unaffordable. The greater the complexity of the car – and the later M5s are very complex indeed – the more of a problem this is likely to be. So it is very important to be realistic before committing yourself to the purchase of a car that is likely to become a major financial commitment. The potential for expensive mistakes is huge, and with an M5 more than almost any other car it is worth paying a specialist to look the car over and prepare a report on it.

Note that the hints on buying and ownership in this chapter cover only the first four generations of BMW M5 – the E28, E34, E39 and E60 models. At the time of writing, the F10 models were still on sale as new cars and it was not possible to compile a sensible list of problem areas.

BUYING AND OWNING AN E28 M5

The E28 M5 was a hand-built car, and it was extremely well built. Most of the problems that are likely to come up will be due either to old age and high mileage or, of course, to neglected maintenance. This first-generation M5 is mercifully less complex that later models, but the newest ones were more than a quarter of a century old by the time this book was written, and they cannot be expected to have the condition of a new car. So saying, an E28 M5 still has the power to thrill.

Body and structure

The bodywork is steel, and it rusts just like that of any other E28 5 Series. Only a very well-kept example will now be completely free of rust, but the good news is that most of the body panels and the structure are the same as on mainstream E28 models and so replacements are not a major problem.

Some rust will be immediately obvious on inspection, and typical areas to be affected are the lower doors, and around the bonnet vents close to the windscreen wipers. Front and rear wheel arches are not immune. It is advisable to check the sunroof panel, and the rear end around the tail-light units and the number-plate lights. The bright metal bumper finishers may rust, too, but this is not a major problem.

The less obvious areas for rust are the sills and jacking points, and the rear bumper mountings. The floorpans can also rust where they meet the sills, and it is important to check this both from under the car and from inside (by lifting the carpets).

One particular problem area is the rear-mounted fuel tank. Water can sit on top of the tank unnoticed for a very long time, and it will eventually rust the tank. Once the tank has been holed, a smell of petrol around the rear of the car is the usual symptom.

It is also wise to check the structure carefully for signs of accident damage, such as rippling in inner panels. There are box-like chassis rails that run below the engine compartment, and these are good indicators of whether a car has been repaired after a front-end shunt.

Interior

Worth noting is that rear legroom is poor on these cars, even though there is plenty of room in the front. They are not therefore well suited to carrying four full-sized adults over long distances.

The M5 badge is universally respected – but of course sometimes deleted by those not keen to advertise the performance potential of their cars. This badge is on an E28 model. MAGIC CAR PICS

SO YOU THINK YOU WANT AN M5?

RIGHT: **The seats in this right-hand-drive E28 M5 are both luxurious and sporting – but above all inviting.** NICK DIMBLEBY

Generally speaking, the interior materials wear well, so signs of damage may indicate that a car has been mistreated. The front seats, and especially that on the driver's side, have side bolsters that may well have become scuffed. This is especially true of the optional Recaro sports seats with their larger bolsters.

Equipment

The E28 M5 was well equipped for its time, but by modern standards borders on the spartan. This is a kind of good news, because it means that there is less special equipment to go wrong.

The electrical system has proved to be robust, and rarely gives trouble unless wires have chafed or earths have been compromised through corrosion. It is always worth checking that electric seat adjustment works properly: if a car has been owned and driven by just one person for a long time, the adjustment mechanism will not have been exercised, and it can seize up. Problems may include debris in the mechanical side of the system, but electrical malfunctions are more likely to be with switches or wiring than with the motors themselves.

Cars that have not been used for a long time may have heater problems. Typical are seized blower motors and tap valves, and condenser failures on cars fitted with air conditioning. On the outside of the car, it is worth checking that the headlamp wipers function correctly, as they are not one of the more robust components and may also only see limited use.

Engine

The 6-cylinder engine is a very strong unit and some experts claim that it is capable of 250,000 miles or more. However, it does

The E28 M5 of course had the classic Motorsport 24-valve 6-cylinder, an engine that is still widely respected today. MAGIC CAR PICS

159

SO YOU THINK YOU WANT AN M5?

require proper maintenance, and that maintenance includes changing the timing chains at intervals of around 100,000 miles.

There are several maladies associated with these chains. The tensioner guides can wear at high mileages, allowing the chain to become slack. The teeth on the crankshaft sprocket also wear eventually, so allowing backlash when the engine is started and allowing the chain to jump a tooth. It is expensive to have the timing chains and associated hardware replaced, but it is very necessary at the prescribed intervals. If the chain jumps a tooth or fails, valves and pistons will come together disastrously and the engine rebuild that follows will be enormously expensive.

Specialists warn of one other common malady, where the engine will not rev beyond about 6,000rpm (the redline is at 6,800rpm). This is actually not an engine fault at all, but is likely to be a problem with the high-pressure in-line fuel supply pump. Engine mountings may also be tired, leading to roughness.

Transmission

The Getrag 280/5 five-speed gearbox was the only one available, and is another long-lived component. It does require regular oil changes, and if these have been skimped there is a greater likelihood of wear – especially if the car has been used hard. It is the synchromesh that suffers first (and is likely to need attention after 150,000 miles or so anyway). Grating noises when changing down the gearbox highlight problems, and are likely to appear on the third to second change initially. In practice, the gearbox will usually soldier on for a long time with worn synchromesh, and this fact discourages owners from having the worn items replaced. Leaks from the gearbox seals are not uncommon, and the seals cannot be replaced unless the gearbox is first removed from the car – time-consuming for even a competent DIY enthusiast and expensive if entrusted to a specialist.

Play in the gear lever is usually nothing worse than worn bushes in the linkages, but a heavy clutch warns that some work is due in that area. Clutch slip can be confirmed under long, hard acceleration. Gearbox mountings deteriorate gradually and may need replacement at high mileages, and if there is roughness in the transmission it is worth examining the propshaft coupling, the centre bearing and even the differential mountings.

Suspension, steering, brakes and wheels

Like many powerful cars with rear-wheel drive, the E28 M5 can be a little tail-happy when provoked. However, that is inherent in the design and does not indicate a problem. A vagueness from the rear end, however, may well be caused by worn mounting bushes on the sub-frame.

Front suspension bushes and ball-joints will wear over time, and a vibration through the steering wheel suggests that the wear has reached unacceptable levels. Replacement of the worn parts is not a massive expense. The centre track rod and the tie rods can wear, and so can the steering arm. Cars for the North American market had self-levelling rear suspension, and this system is prone to leaks. If the rear tyres rub against the bodywork when the car is laden, or if they wear oddly, the chances are that there is a problem here. The system is expensive to rebuild and some owners have removed it, replacing it with standard suspension components from an E28 535i.

If the steering feels heavier in one direction than the other, the steering box is probably worn, and might even have partially seized. However, it is worth changing the filter at the bottom of the PAS fluid reservoir before assuming the worst. If this becomes blocked, it can cause strange steering maladies.

The car should obviously come to a halt smoothly and in a straight line. If there is judder from the brakes, the discs may be warped – a quite common problem, especially on cars that have been used hard. Seized calipers may also be

Stylish alloy wheels are now standard wear on most BMW models, but the M5 had them from the start in 1984. These are the style associated with the E28 or first-generation cars. MAGIC CAR PICS

SO YOU THINK YOU WANT AN M5?

found on cars that have been unused for a time; the calipers are not found on other E34 models (they are shared with the M635 CSi coupé) and are expensive to replace, although they can usually be reconditioned.

All the E28 M5s have ABS, and this has its own warning light on the dashboard. (It is worth checking that the light comes on before the engine is started; if not, has the bulb been removed to hide a fault?) If the light is on permanently, the ABS pump or control unit may have failed, or corroded wheel sensors may be giving a false reading.

Early E28 M5s outside North America came with metric (Michelin TRX) wheels, and these take tyres of a special size that are not easy to find and can be expensive. As a result, many owners have fitted the alternative cross-spoke wheels that do take standard-sized tyres. The condition of the wheels does matter: kerbing damage is unsightly at the very least, and it is neither easy nor cheap to find the correct replacements.

BUYING AND OWNING AN E34 M5

Even though the early 3.6-litre and later 3.8-litre variants of the E34 M5 are dealt with in separate chapters in this book, they can comfortably be discussed together here. Like the E28s, the E34s were hand-built by the BMW Motorsport division (or BMW M, as it was called after 1993) and they were superbly put together, so most problems are the result of old age, misuse or neglect. Many M5 enthusiasts rate the E34 models as the best of all, not least because of their good looks, and the 3.8-litre models as the best of the best.

Body and structure

Most body panels are standard E34 items, which means that rust in wings and door bottoms need not be a particular problem. However, the rustier a car appears on the outside, the greater the chance that there is hidden rust elsewhere.

The front wings, wheel arches and grille panel can all rust. The sills and jacking points are also vulnerable, although they are not easy to see underneath the plastic trims. The fuel filler recess, the rear wheel arches and even the boot lid can also suffer. Another area to check is the base of the windscreen, where the metalwork will rust if a replacement windscreen has not been properly bonded to its frame. The boot lid can rust around the spoiler mountings (where one is fitted), and that spoiler can also damage the paint on the tops of the rear wings.

The sunroof needs occasional lubrication, or it is likely to seize. Some Touring models were supplied with a double sunroof, in which the opening mechanism of the two is linked. If this is fitted, check that it operates correctly, as it notoriously does not. The operation of the two roofs is synchronized, and failures are often caused when this synchronization is lost. In these cases, straightforward adjustment (by somebody who understands the system) is the cure.

BMW does much of its testing at the Nürburgring, where this 3.8-litre E34 M5 was pictured. Many owners gain huge enjoyment from track-day events with their cars. BMW

■ SO YOU THINK YOU WANT AN M5?

That badge again ... The spoiler was optional, and many owners chose not to have it. The car is a 3.8-litre E34 M5. BMW

Interior

Like the E28 models, these cars have ample room in the front but a disappointing amount of legroom in the rear. The seats normally wear well, although of course the bolsters on the driver's seat will become scuffed and worn over time. Most cars were built with leather upholstery, which is easy enough to have replaced by a professional trimmer. However, the cloth upholstery is much harder to replace if it becomes damaged or stained – and the light grey variety does seem to mark easily. It is important to check that the electric adjustment for the front seats works as it should, as components tend to seize if left in one setting for a long time.

In the front footwells, check for damp carpets, which will often give themselves away by their smell. These typically result from a leaking windscreen, blocked sunroof drain tubes, or leaks from the heater matrix or air conditioning system. Another worthwhile check is to lift the rear seat and inspect the area around the battery; corrosion caused by acid spills or leaks may affect the electrical components located there, among them the control unit for the EDC on the 3.8-litre cars.

On the dashboard, make sure that there are no missing pixels on the read-out from the on-board computer or in the mileage display. These may seem like minor failures, but in worst cases they can make the read-outs impossible to decipher, and they can be quite tricky to put right. The service interval indicator lights can sometimes give trouble – an early example of a convenience feature that was more trouble than it was worth, in some expert opinions. The heater control panel can fail, and is not cheap to replace, and of course the air conditioning should work properly. Compressor and condenser alike can fail if they are not regularly used.

Equipment

The E34 models were still relatively free of 'technology toys', so there is not a lot to look for in this area. However, whatever is fitted should work! One particular problem, which results in all kinds of spurious warning lights on the dash, is associated with the rear wiring harness. On both saloon and Touring models, the harness passes through the hinge for the boot (or tailgate), where it can chafe, and bare wires may come together. This problem is found particularly on the Touring models.

Neat and functional, with supportive and adjustable seats, this is the interior of a UK-market E34 3.8-litre car. That proliferation of buttons on the centre stack eventually pushed BMW into designing its iDrive system. BMW GB

SO YOU THINK YOU WANT AN M5?

This is the 3.6-litre version of the S38 engine from an E34 model. These engines were already complex enough. BMW

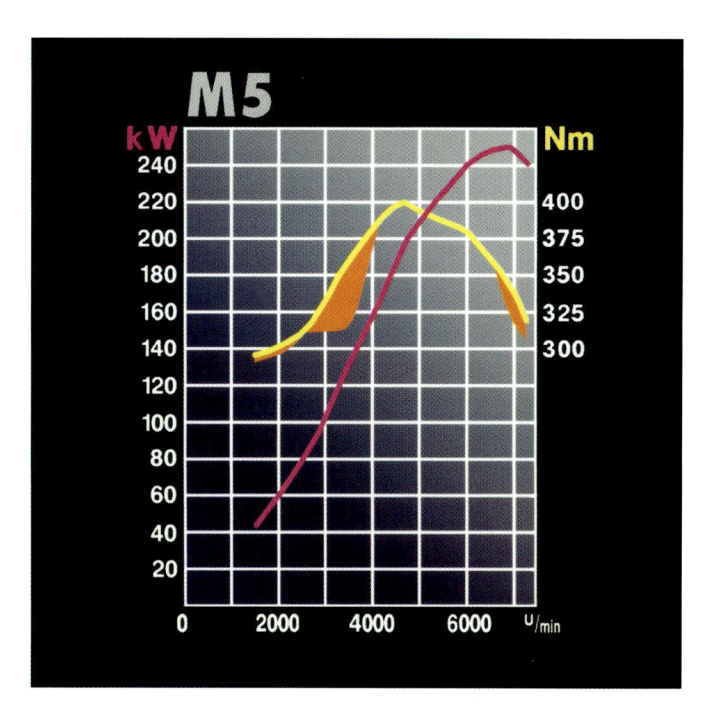

These are the statistics that give the M5 its character, as seen on the power and torque graph for the 3.8-litre engine in an E34 model. The power figures here are expressed in kW (Kilowatts) rather than the more common PS (Pferdestärke, or horsepower calculated to German DIN standards). BMW

Engine

The 3.6-litre and 3.8-litre engines in the E34 cars share their basic design with the 3.5-litre engine in the E28. Like that engine, they are long-lived and robust if properly maintained, and mileages of over 200,000 are not uncommon. Also like the earlier engine, they need top-quality oil and they need to have their timing chain changed at about 100,000 miles. The duplex chain does not otherwise give any particular trouble, but a popular enthusiast modification is to fit the stronger chain tensioner from the E36 M3 engine.

The engine has to come out for the timing chain to be replaced, and so it makes good sense to have seals and other items replaced at the same time. The bill will be that much larger, but the peace of mind that much greater. Cheapskate owners skimp on these things, leaving problems for others to sort out later. Also often missed in order to save money is the regular check of valve clearances. Shims are used to set the clearances, and this obviously has to be done with the engine cold.

The 24-valve Motorsport 'six' was still the M5's power unit until the end of E34 production. This is a 3.8-litre type. MAGIC CAR PICS

163

■ SO YOU THINK YOU WANT AN M5?

Oil leaks are quite common on high-mileage engines, particularly from the front cover, the sump, the back of the head gasket and the cam carrier. Many owners ignore these until the leaks become a real problem, because a quite extensive (and therefore expensive) strip-down is often necessary to locate and rectify them properly. The cooling system also deserves a thorough check, to prevent disastrous overheating. The condition of hoses is obviously important, but thermostats can fail, water pumps can leak, and the viscous coupling for the engine fan can also not operate correctly. As for exhausts, these may well last for 100,000 miles, but the catalytic converter probably will not and is very expensive. Beware of rattles from the 'cat': it is not unknown for owners to remove the internal components and weld the casing together again, but of course no car so treated will pass its emissions test.

The accelerator should operate smoothly and without sticking, but it may feel quite stiff to those used to more modern machinery. On these engines, it still uses a cable to open the throttles – and there are six of them to open here.

Transmission

As in the E28 M5, the 3.6-litre and early 3.8-litre cars have a five-speed Getrag gearbox; the late 3.8-litre models have a Getrag six-speed type. Neither is especially troublesome, but when problems do arise they are likely to be expensive ones.

A floppy gearshift will probably be nothing worse than worn linkages, which are not expensive to rectify. Oil leaks from the rear of the gearbox are also common, but again not expensive to rectify – unless, that is, the gearbox has to come out for all the seals to be replaced. If there is a rattle from the gearbox at idle (when the clutch pedal is not depressed), suspect a worn layshaft bearing – which might or might not carry on for a long time without further problems. Graunching noises on downshifts mean the synchromesh is

M5s sold well on the European continent, and there is no reason not to buy a car delivered new in another country – unless its left-hand drive is a deterrent in right-hand-drive UK, for example. However, there were minor differences to suit different markets, and it is advisable to check carefully whether modifications are required when importing a car. This is a French-market E34 3.8-litre. BMW FRANCE

worn, but again this will not interfere with the actual functioning of the gearbox.

As on the E28s, the clutch should not be heavy, and heaviness is a warning that it needs to be changed. In a worst case, it can break up and cause expensive damage to the flywheel and the engine sensors around it. A vibration under acceleration suggests that the propshaft coupling or centre bearing has failed.

As on any car, clunks or rumbles from the differential are bad news, but differential oil leaks can usually be tolerated unless they are severe.

Suspension, steering, brakes and wheels

If the car patters over bumps in the road, the dampers are past their best. Leaks from the rear dampers are a very bad sign as these are an integral part of the EDC system and are very expensive to replace. Some owners have replaced the EDC system with non-adjustable dampers simply to avoid the bills associated with EDC failure.

Front suspension components wear at high mileages or from misuse. Clunks and rattles from the front end over uneven surfaces warn of wear in the upper ball-joints, and straight-line shimmy at about 50mph is caused by wear in the bushes of the upper and lower control arms. Vague steering comes from worn ball-joints on the track rods, while pitch or lurch in corners suggests that the anti-roll bar linkages are worn out. At the rear, when the driven wheels try to steer the car, the problem is likely to be worn rear sub-frame mounting bushes, which will need to be replaced every 100,000 miles or so anyway.

Brake discs last around 40,000 miles. When checking a car for sale, it is worth looking carefully at the condition of the brake pipes as well, because replacement is quite a complicated job and is accompanied by a big bill.

Wear on the inner edges of the front tyres is another indicator of worn suspension ball-joints, and other instances of odd tyre wear will certainly be caused by a suspension problem of some sort. Wheels can of course suffer from kerbing damage, but can be refurbished at a cost; better-quality tyres have rim protectors moulded into their sidewalls. More of a worry is when the wheel covers ('turbine' on the 3.6 and 'throwing star' on the 3.8) are damaged or missing, because these outer sections of the two-piece wheels are quite hard to find on their own and the whole wheel may have to be replaced.

BUYING AND OWNING AN E39 M5

The E39 model became the most numerous version of the M5 yet, which means that there are likely to be many to

At the time of writing, many M5 enthusiasts considered the E39 model to be the best of them all. Lacking some of the complexity of the later models, it comes with a rewarding soundtrack from its V8 engine. BMW

SO YOU THINK YOU WANT AN M5?

choose from for some time to come. All were saloons, which simplifies the choice, and all came with the same 5-litre V8 engine and six-speed manual gearbox. These cars were not built by hand in the BMW M workshops, but were assembled on the main assembly lines that also turned out everyday variants of the E39. They were also extraordinarily capable, although they heralded a new era in which advanced technology would increasingly complicate the ownership experience for those without unlimited funds.

Body and structure

Rust is not as much of a problem on these cars as on earlier M5s, although it is certainly not absent altogether. An annoying but cosmetic rust problem affects the window frames, where rust will bubble up under the black finish, typically near the bottom of the frames. More serious is rust in a seam on the front underside of the bonnet, near the headlights, and the underside of the boot lid can also rust along a seam where its two sections are joined. The fuel filler recess, which typically misses out when the car is cleaned, can also begin to rust.

As always, any ripples in the metal understructure of the car, poor panel fits or poor paint matches suggest that the car has been in a major accident and that repairs have been carried out cheaply. This in turn suggests that other areas of maintenance may have been skimped.

Interior

The interiors are generally hard-wearing, although the extended and complete leather versions have more leather to become scuffed and torn. Excessive interior damage means the car has had a hard life and will warn of likely problems elsewhere.

Seat bolsters are usually the first to succumb to wear, but the leather is generally long-lasting. Some of the coloured leathers seem to show wear more readily on the seat cushions than others. Check that the electric seat adjustment works properly, because components do seize up after long periods of inactivity.

As on the E34 models, a quite common problem is missing pixels in the digital information panels on the dashboard. This can often be quite expensive to put right, so owners may not bother unless it starts causing real problems.

Some cars have a satellite navigation system, but it is worth remembering that this is quite crude by the standards of even the cheaper modern systems. For that reason, owners may choose not to have it repaired if it fails. If the ABS warning light is permanently lit on the dashboard, the ABS pump or control unit may have failed, or there may be a problem with one or more of the wheel sensors. In all cases, make sure that the light does illuminate as a check when the ignition is on; owners do remove the bulb to hide faults.

Further important checks focus on the heating and air-conditioning systems. Heater control modules can fail altogether, but can at least be replaced by a competent DIY enthusiast. The air conditioning should deliver cold air, and if it does not then either the dryer or the condenser has probably failed. As the standard fit is an automatic climate control system that is dependent on sensors, a failure to respond to settings may result from a temperature sensor problem.

Equipment

Equipment levels vary from car to car so much that it is impossible to give a complete run-down of likely problems here. The most important advice is to check that everything fitted to the car actually works before committing to a purchase.

Two common problems worth mentioning affect the Park Distance Control and the power-folding door mirrors. If the Park Distance Control malfunctions, the likelihood is that its sensors (in the rear bumper apron and sometimes the front apron as well) are at fault. Sometimes, the problem is nothing more than dirt obscuring the face of a sensor. The door mirrors are operated by motors, and these motors can fail.

Engine

The S62B50 is a much-respected engine, with enough torque to give plenty of flexibility at low speeds as well as a menacing V8 rumble that rises to a race-like howl at high speeds. Fuel economy is quite reasonable, and although a lot of town work or heavy use of the performance will give consumption of 15mpg or less, it is possible to get 23mpg or better in long steady-speed cruising.

However, it is a very complex engine, and really should be checked over by a specialist before you commit to buying a car. The most expensive problems come from failures of the Double-VANOS system, which fortunately has a good reliability if the engine is properly maintained. Do not be worried by a rattle on starting the engine, which should go away after fifteen seconds or so as the oil circulates round the engine. If the rattle is still there after a minute or more, there is a problem. This may be accompanied by the engine management warning light on the dashboard remaining illuminated. (As always, make sure that it does come on as part of the check cycle and has not been disabled to disguise a problem.)

These engines also drink oil. They were designed with low-friction piston rings, and a certain amount of oil gets blown past these rings in normal use. On early engines, the loss of a litre every 500 miles or so is quite normal; after 2000, redesigned rings reduced this loss but did not eliminate it. Higher consumption is a cause for concern, but of course may come from leaks. The sump gasket and rocker cover gaskets are known to develop leaks, and owners may not bother to replace them because of the associated cost. Oil can also leak from around the filter housing.

Other known problems, which usually result in an illuminated engine warning light, are in the position sensors used on the crankshaft and camshafts. In addition, the Mass Airflow Meters can become choked, and this can reduce engine performance quite noticeably. As for the exhaust system, it deserves a thorough check because replacements are expensive. The two catalytic converters are particularly so, and as on the E34s, unscrupulous owners have been known to remove the internal components as a short-term 'fix' for a worn-out or poisoned catalytic converter.

Transmission

The gearbox in the E39 M5 is essentially the same tough Getrag six-speed type that was used in the final E34 models. It does not normally give trouble, although wear after high mileages is inevitable. As on earlier M5s, a heavy clutch pedal warns of problems, and a worn clutch can break up and destroy the flywheel and associated sensors. As the flywheel on the V8 engine is a dual-mass type, it is particularly expensive.

As on other M5 models, the differential may leak oil. As long as this is a drip rather than a torrent, and as long as the oil is kept topped up at regular intervals, this should not be a big problem.

This is that V8 engine. As always the under-bonnet view was impressive and attractive, but maintenance required skill, or preferably a specialist. TERABASS/WIKIMEDIA

Suspension, steering, brakes and wheels

Hard use leads to premature wear in the suspension, so draw your own conclusions if there are several problems. Steering wheel vibration is the usual indicator of wear in the front suspension components, typically anti-roll bar links, thrust arm bushes or ball-joints. At the rear, the mounting brackets for the anti-roll bar are a known weakness, and some owners have converted to stronger aftermarket items.

The steering is quick, but despite BMW M's best efforts it is not as sharp as a rack-and-pinion system. As for the brakes, vibration points to wear, and that may mean that the car has been used hard or that maintenance has been neglected. Neither is a good sign.

Like all large-diameter alloy wheels, those on the M5 can suffer from kerbing damage, and the rear tyres will wear out quickly if the full performance is used a lot. Once again, they can be a good indicator of the way a car has been treated and of how well it has been maintained.

BUYING AND OWNING AN E60 OR E61 M5

To some extent, these fourth-generation M5 models have proved controversial, mainly because of their complexity.

■ SO YOU THINK YOU WANT AN M5?

One of the delights of an M5 is that it was designed to be capable of this kind of use on the track. However, it does not have to be used like that ... BMW

When all the various systems and items of equipment are in the peak of health, the cars are very impressive pieces of machinery. However, all these systems need regular maintenance checks; some are prone to annoying failures (often caused by wiring problems); and cars that have not been maintained to a high standard can be a liability. It takes both money and care to keep an E60 or E61 M5 in the style to which its makers intended it to become accustomed.

Where many other cars still have fixed servicing schedules, the E60 and E61 M5s do not. Instead, the iDrive and DIS systems calculate how the car has been driven, what needs to be serviced and when. However, replacement of some consumable items can be predicted, at least roughly.

It is always worth looking at the iDrive service schedule to find out what maintenance work is likely to be necessary in the near future. BMW dealers can actually interrogate the car's electronic systems to find out such things as how often the Launch Control has been used, which is a good indicator of whether the car has been systematically abused – and some cars have.

Body and structure

The bodyshells of these cars had not revealed major weaknesses at the time of writing, and one reason for that may be that the normally vulnerable front end is made of aluminium

... because all models of M5 are fully usable as everyday transport. This US-specification E60 with its hugely powerful V10 engine is being used for precisely that. BMW

alloy (which was chosen to get the right weight balance, not for its resistance to corrosion). So although stone damage on the nose may look unsightly, and although the headlights are prone to misting up if water gets past their seals, there is not a lot to worry about – yet. One problem that has arisen is with the sunroof, which can sometimes create a good deal of wind noise. Correct adjustment is usually the cure.

The E61 Touring models are essentially the same as the E60 saloons, but they do have a few problems of their own. The automatic opening and closing function of the tailgate is one of these. The opening switch for the tailgate glass can suffer from water ingress, with inevitable results, and a wiring fault may cause the tailgate or the glass section to unlock or open at random. This problem is often associated with a dashboard warning of high drain on the battery.

The power-operated load space blind may also stick, a fault usually caused by its screw drive mechanism rather than the motor itself. Finally, the rear washer may fail, which is typically caused by a detached or blocked water pipe. When rectifying this, it is as well to make sure that the washer has not been dumping large quantities of water into the well where the spare tyre and tools are kept, because the multiple electronic items mounted there may be affected.

Interior

The upholstery and interior fittings of the E60 and E61 cars had proved typically robust by the time of writing. However, some owners have reported squeaking noises from the active seats that can be hard to track down. On a car equipped with the ventilated seats (identified by perforated leather on the cushion and backrest) it is important to check whether the ventilation function works properly. Realistically, it will hardly spoil your driving enjoyment if it does not, but it can be a useful bargaining point.

Owners have reported a number of troubles with the dashboard warning lights, and these seem to be entirely typical of the electrical maladies to which these cars are prone. A common problem is false-alarm warning lights for the airbags, and the seat belt warning light can sometimes warn that a belt has not been fastened, even when the relevant seat is unoccupied. Multiple fault lights that came up on some early cars were caused by a faulty steering angle sensor: the various systems on these cars are so interdependent that one simple fault may have several unexpected outcomes.

Equipment

In the early days of the E60 and E61 M5s owners reported a large number of electrical problems, many of them resulting in the false-alarm dashboard warning lights already mentioned. BMW was obliged to develop some updated software, which could be downloaded to the cars by authorized dealers and cured most of the problems. However, the cars' early reputation still lingers on.

When looking over a potential purchase, remember to check as many of the different functions as you can. This requires patience. It also requires patience to get to understand some of these systems in order to get the most out of them. The iDrive, for example, is simply baffling without a long and careful read of the owner's manual. Once it is set up to suit your preferences, its value becomes clearer. However, every owner has different preferences and therefore different settings, and the cars also adapt their responses to a degree to the driver's style. This is why no two cars will drive alike. It is important to make allowances for this when looking over possible purchases.

Engine

The complicated V10 engine has a sound like no other, and that is addictive. It might also lead you into parting with your cash before completing all the necessary checks. Bear in mind, too, that you really will have to visit petrol stations more regularly than with many other cars, thanks to a small (70-litre, 15-gallon) fuel tank that gives a range of only about 200 miles between refills. As for fuel consumption, expect about 17–18mpg overall. The figure may drop alarmingly in town work, to around 10–12mpg, but gentle motorway use should give about 23–24mpg. Fuel consumption will obviously be worse if the car is used hard, and single figures are within the experience of many enthusiastic owners. Worth remembering is that the V10 does not take kindly to too much pottering around town and really does need a good blast once in a while to keep it in top condition.

Generally, though, the engine seems to be robust – with the possible exception of the Double-VANOS system. Early engines had an oil pipe that could not take the high pressure used for this version of VANOS, but most will have had the pipe replaced under warranty. This is fortunate, as a great deal of dismantling is involved to reach it. Even in top condition, the V10 uses some oil, and you should expect

SO YOU THINK YOU WANT AN M5?

With the V10 engine, BMW stepped outside the bounds of most drivers' experiences. The under-bonnet view is beautiful, but costs can be very high indeed. BMW

to add a litre every 3,000 miles or so – or more often if the car is used hard. Note that BMW demands a special specification of oil, and that the use of any other kind will invalidate whatever warranty the car may still have. When checking over a potential purchase, it is worth looking for oil leaks from the engine, although these are difficult to see from above because the whole power unit is hidden under a plastic cosmetic cover.

Transmission

Not everybody likes the SMG gearbox on these cars, which can give harsh changes when driven hard and can sometimes give jerky control in traffic. The alternative six-speed manual gearbox was available only in North America and seems to have no special vices. Its main advantage is probably that it removes the worries associated with SMG failure and, in the right hands, can smooth out progress in town traffic.

Very expensive problems can also affect the SMG gearbox. Problems are signalled first by an orange gearwheel symbol on the dash, and this is succeeded by a red one, which is known to enthusiast owners as the Red Cog of Death. Sometimes it is produced by a wiring fault, but its real function is to warn of SMG failure – in the control unit, the pump or the clutch position sensor.

Central to the SMG is a hydraulic pump that operates the clutch, and this can fail; early cars were especially prone to the problem and many had replacement pumps under warranty. An improved pump (and revised control software) was fitted from 2007. The clutch itself has problems if it judders as the car moves off from rest; typically, the clutch release bearing and its guide bush have run dry and are not releasing properly. Clutches normally last between 40,000 and 50,000 miles, but their life expectancy is considerably reduced if the car is driven hard and the Launch Control is used a lot. Replacements are very expensive.

A quiet, high-pitched whining noise from the differential is quite normal for these cars, and results from the design of the differential. Similarly, a low grinding noise at car park speeds, especially on a tight right-hand lock, is not as bad as it sounds: it is caused by friction between the lined disc and the steel disc within the limited-slip mechanism. If the differential oil is replaced with a special type available from BMW, the noise should disappear – but experts say that it might take several hundred miles before the new oil works its magic and the noise goes away altogether.

Obviously, excessive differential noise of any kind is a cause for concern and, as it is not unknown for the differential seals to leak, it is wise to keep an eye open for oil drips where a car has been parked.

Suspension, steering, brakes and wheels

Listen carefully for knocking noises from the suspension on an E60 or E61 M5. A knock at the front might be nothing worse than a loose securing bolt for the front strut tower brace, but obviously suspension wear is possible if the car has done a high mileage. At the rear, a knocking noise typically comes from loose or broken top mounts on the dampers.

Check for vibrations through the steering column and noise from the front end when cornering, both of which may indicate that there is wear in the front control arms. These last around 20,000 miles before needing replacement, but are fortunately not hugely expensive.

These were the first M5s to have rack-and-pinion steering, which should be quick and sharp. Any suspicion of vagueness deserves careful investigation.

A humming noise from the discs under braking is quite normal for all cars with cross-drilled discs like those on the E60 and E61. The discs last between 30,000 and 40,000

SO YOU THINK YOU WANT AN M5?

miles, but are due for replacement when a lip appears around their edges. Discolouration of the discs is a warning sign that the car has been used hard and that the brakes have got very hot, and it is not unknown for discs to crack. Vibration under braking will also suggest that disc replacement is due. It is expensive to replace a full set of four, but top-quality brakes are essential on a car with the M5's performance. Brake pads usually last for about 15,000 miles, but less in hard use.

As always, check for kerbing damage to the alloy wheels, which are inevitably expensive to replace. As for tyres, those on the rear can be expected to last for between 10,000 and 15,000 miles, while those on the front wheels should last rather longer. Heavily worn rear tyres are of course an indication of both hard use and of an owner who has stopped spending money on keeping the car in tip-top condition.

Recent M5s have showcased a great deal of advanced technology, and among their features have been the two-piece design of the brake discs seen here. This type of technology is one reason why initial purchase and later maintenance of an M5 can be very expensive. BMW

Although early M5s were invariably discreet, the more recent cars have been available with more eye-catching colour schemes. Nobody could miss this Frozen Red paint contrasting with black wheels on a 2012 M Performance Edition. BMW

■ SO YOU THINK YOU WANT AN M5?

Inviting, and somewhat slick as well, this is the driving compartment of a UK-market F10 M5. BMW GB

The under-bonnet scene in an F10 M5 exudes power, although the engine's presentation seems strangely untidy compared to that of some earlier M5 models. BMW

SO YOU THINK YOU WANT AN M5?

Labelled with the name of its manufacturers, Getrag, this is the seven-speed DCT gearbox of an F10 model. It contains a great deal of sophisticated technology and, like so much modern equipment, depends on electronic controls. BMW

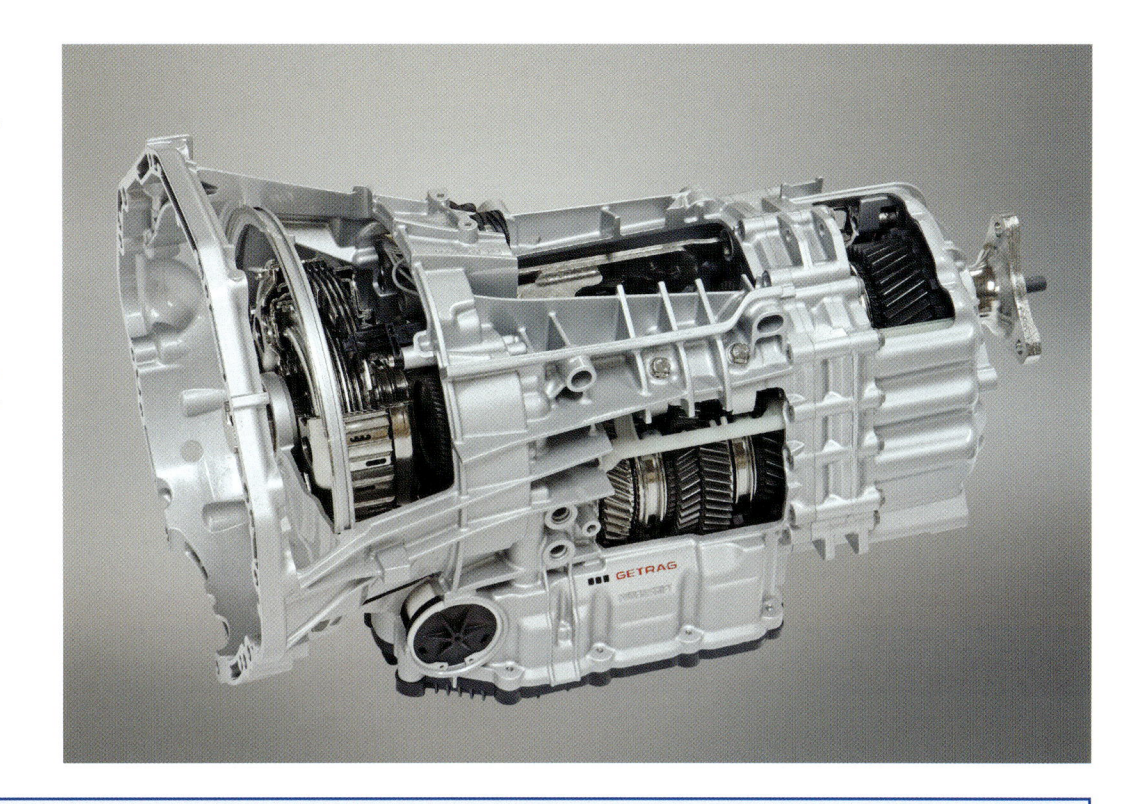

M5 VIN CODES

The individual type codes for M5 models are shown in each chapter, but it is helpful to see how these fit into the overall pattern of the car's VIN code.

The full VIN code ('chassis number') is found on a metal plate visible through the base of the windscreen and is also stamped around the front suspension tower. It should match the number on the registration or ownership documents!

VIN codes have 17 characters, and it is characters 4–7 that are normally used to identify an M5 variant (e.g. HC91 for a European E34 3.8-litre, or NB93 for a North American E60). The full alphanumeric string can be interpreted as follows:

Character(s)	Example	Meaning
1–3	WBS	Manufactured by BMW Motorsport (later BMW M). Note that some very early E28 M5s had the WBA code associated with mainstream BMW models
4–5	HC	Type code (*see the listings in Chapters 2 to 7*)
6	9	M5 model
7	2	Variant (1 = European LHD, 2 = RHD, 3 = North American specification)
8	2	Restraint system (2 = driver and passenger front airbags)
9	7	Randomly generated check digit, designed to prevent fraud (may be 0–9 or X)
10	A	Model-year
11	B	Assembly plant code
12–17	123456	Serial number

INDEX

Alpina   7, 9
AMG   7

BMW M (name change)   22, 76
building the first M5s   33

car type code numbers   21

DCT transmission   141
Dingolfing (factory)   16, 88

E28 M5, announcement   24
 assembly   36
 buying and owning   158
 Canadian cars   38
 interior   30
 Japanese cars   39
 North American cars   37
 paint and upholstery options   42
 powertrain   28
 press opinions   35
 production totals   41
 RHD cars   34
 South African cars   39
 specifications   44
 steering, suspension and brakes   30
E28 mainstream models   23
E34 M5, 20 Jahre Motorsport Edition   77
 announcement   48
 buying and owning   161
 Cecotto Edition   59
 Elekta Edition   78
 exterior features, 3.8   69
 interior   52, 70
 Japanese cars   57
 Middle East cars   57
 Naghi Motors Edition   59

North American cars   55, 57
paint and upholstery options   61, 82, 83
performance figures   60, 80
powertrain   49, 67
press opinions   55, 76
production changes, 3.6-litre cars   54
production changes, 3.8-litre cars   74
production totals   60, 80
revised chassis, 3.8-litre cars   68
RHD cars   54, 76
South African cars   57
special editions   59, 76
specifications   64, 81
steering, suspension and brakes   51
Touring models   72
UK Limited Edition   77
Winkelhock Edition   59
E34 mainstream models   45
E35 M5 convertible   57
E39 M5, buying and owning   165
 Canadian cars   99
 creation   87
 interior   94
 North American cars   99
 paint and upholstery options   102
 performance figures   100
 powertrain   89
 press opinions   98
 production changes   97
 production totals   100
 RHD cars   98
 specifications   101
 steering, suspension and brakes   92
 Touring prototype   88
E39 mainstream models   84
E60 mainstream models   105
E60 & E61, 25th Anniversary Edition   125

INDEX

buying and owning 167
CSL concept 127
customising the driving experience 118
engine 110
exterior design 107
gearbox 115
interior 119
interior trim options 128
North American cars 124
paint options 130
performance figures 128
press opinions 123
production changes 121
production totals 128
RHD cars 124
special editions 125
specifications 129
steering, suspension and brakes 92
Touring (E61) 121
upholstery options 132
engine type code numbers 21

F10 M5, 30 Jahre Edition 151
driving dynamics 142
engine 139
exterior 136
interior 143
M Performance Edition 147
Nighthawk Edition 151
North American cars 146
paint and interior options 156
performance figures 154
press opinions 148
production changes 146
RHD cars 146
special editions 147
specifications 155

transmission 142
F10 mainstream models 134
frozen paints 147
future M5 18

Garching (Motorsport plant) 16, 35

M1 11, 13
M5 and motor sport 12
M535i (E12) 10
M535i (E28) 10
M88 engine 14
M brand 13
Michelin TRX wheels and tyres 33
Mercedes-Benz 14, 16, 22, 45, 65, 85
Motorsport 5 Series cars 9

North America, importance 18

Opel 14, 45, 65

performance comparison, five generations of M5 20
Preussenstrasse plant 35

Ring Taxi 22

S38 engine 14
SMG gearbox 115
South African CKD 10, 39

timeline for M5 19
Twin Power Turbo engine 139

V10 Formula 1 engine 113
Valvetronic 140
Vauxhall Lotus Carlton 45, 65
VIN codes 173

RELATED TITLES FROM CROWOOD

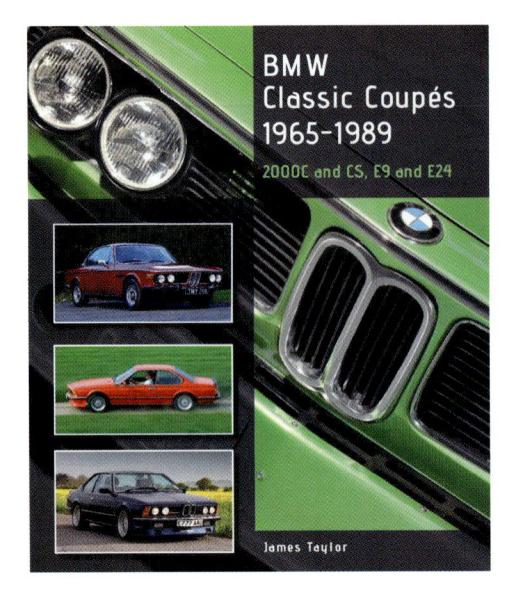

BMW Classic Coupés 1969–1989
JAMES TAYLOR
ISBN 978 1 84797 846 2
192pp, 230 illustrations

BMW M3
JAMES TAYLOR
ISBN 978 1 84797 772 4
192pp, 250 illustrations

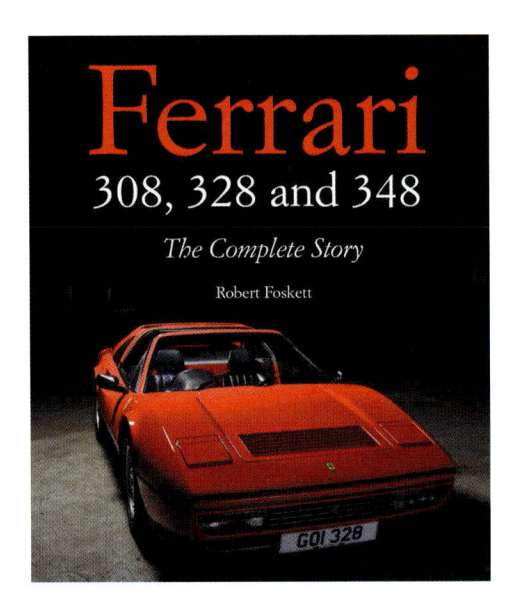

Ferrari 308, 328 and 348
ROBERT FOSKETT
ISBN 978 1 84797 885 1
192pp, 300 illustrations

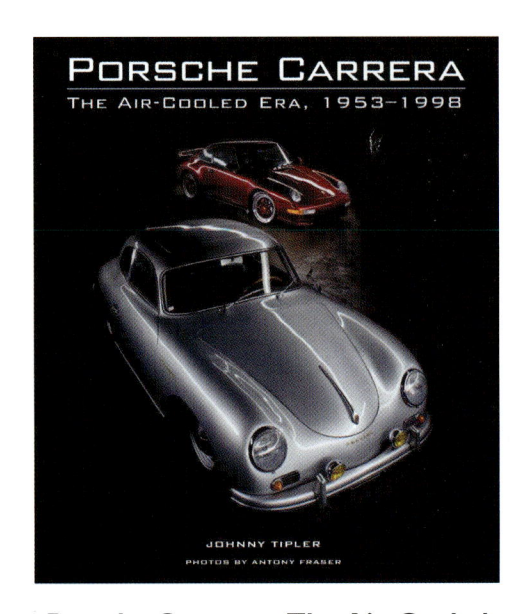

Porsche Carrera – The Air-Cooled Era, 1953–1998
JOHNNY TIPLER
ISBN 978 1 84797 669 4
272pp, 400 illustrations

In case of difficulty ordering, please contact the Sales Office:

The Crowood Press, Ramsbury, Wiltshire SN8 2HR UK

Tel: 44 (0) 1672 520320   enquiries@crowood.com   www.crowood.com